IMAGES
of America

BIG HORN CITY

ON THE COVER: BIG HORN MERC, MARCH 1884. John Sackett and Charles Skinner's Big Horn Mercantile was built in 1882. The sign above the door reads, "Big Horn Post Office." It was the first mercantile established in what is now Sheridan County. Pictured from left to right are O.P. Benefield, John W. Austin, William E. Jackson, Charles Farwell, Carl Sackett (young boy), John H. Sackett (left in doorway), Charles W. Skinner (right in doorway), two unidentified (could be Tom Tynan sitting on the wooden box), Oliver P. Hanna, two Wolfe boys, J.W. Wolfe, and an unidentified man on a horse. The child in the upper left window is a Sackett boy. (George Harper and family in honor of Charles Skinner's granddaughter Mary.)

IMAGES
of America

BIG HORN CITY

Judy Slack, Bozeman Trail Museum,
Big Horn City Historical Society

ARCADIA
PUBLISHING

Published by Arcadia Publishing
Charleston, South Carolina

Library of Congress Control Number: 2010928307

For all general information, please contact Arcadia Publishing:
Telephone 843-853-2070
Fax 843-853-0044
E-mail sales@arcadiapublishing.com
For customer service and orders:
Toll-Free 1-888-313-2665

Visit us on the Internet at www.arcadiapublishing.com

To the current and former volunteers of the Big Horn City Historical Society; the pioneer families; the Sheridan County Fulmer Public Library, Wyoming Room; and the University of Wyoming, American Heritage Center for preserving our history and sharing it with us in this book.

CONTENTS

ACKNOWLEDGMENTS

I would like to thank the Big Horn City Historical Society for allowing me to use its photograph collection in the Bozeman Trail Museum and for sponsoring this book project. I especially want to thank the pioneer family descendants who shared their photographs: Gary McCoy; Donna Eckerson Angel; Victor Garber; Roy Garber; Tempe Javitz; George Harper; Tom Harper; Jim Townsend; Trish Genereaux Coffeen and her sons Christopher, Nathan, and Quinn; Inga McCoy; Bert Dow; Paddy Bard; Chuck Custis; John Zullig; Georgia Torland; Zane Hilman; John Custis; and Marce Lee Nelson. I greatly appreciate Marilyn Bilyeu for sharing the Elsa Spear Byron Collection with us and making it available at the Wyoming Room. The staff of the Wyoming Room at the Sheridan County Fulmer Public Library—Karen Woinoski and Andy Wenburg—were of great help in the search for photographs and news articles.

Our book was also enhanced with the sharing of photographs by the Big Horn Fire Department, D.J. Purcell and Kay Wallick, Mona Coates Brown, Big Horn Woman's Club, Bob Rolston, Dan Berry, Ed Schunk, Deck Hunter, Bob and Joan Wallick, Dana Prater at the Sheridan County Museum, Melvine Rolston, Tom Logan, John and Janet Berry, the Nickerson family, Ann Gorzalka, Robert Legoski, Charlie Popovich, Tom Ringley, Scott Burgan, Carolyn Badgett, Stan Woinoski, and Wyla, Dennis, and Marion Loomis.

Others who helped with the captions and verified facts were Donna Eckerson Angel and the author's brothers, Jim and John Currie. Editing was a monumental job performed by Pat Best. Others who volunteered information or financial assistance were Daryl and Jean Daly, Helen Graham, John and Shirley Genereaux, Bob and Shirley Genereaux, Frances Genereaux Hansen, Patty Warner, Forrest Mars, Toby Thobaben, and Mary Ellen McWilliams.

The Big Horn City Historical Society Board of Directors was a huge support. Board members are Meshelle Powell, Mona Brown, Elaine Hilman, Mike Kuzara, Patty Gingles, and Polly Hill, and museum assistant Maureen Badgett.

An attempt was made to give the appropriate credit for each photograph. The following abbreviations are used for photograph sources: BHCHS-BTM (Big Horn City Historical Society–Bozeman Trail Museum); CHIEF, INC. (Coffeen Historical Information Education Foundation, Inc.); DH Vol. No. (Deck Hunter's Big Horn City books volume number); JS (Judy Slack, the book's author), SCM (Sheridan County Museum); and WYRM (Wyoming Room at the Sheridan County Fulmer Public Library).

Royalties from the sale of this book will benefit the Bozeman Trail Museum located in the Blacksmith Shop in Big Horn, Wyoming.

The responsibility for any errors or omissions rests with the author. This book could not have been completed without the encouragement of my family, especially my husband, John. And a very special thank you to my mother, Helen Currie, who worked so hard on the museum collection.

INTRODUCTION

Dr. Joe Medicine Crow, a respected tribal historian, presented a program about the history of the Crow tribe to the Big Horn City Historical Society at the Big Horn Woman's Club in March 2005. He was 92 at the time. Below, his speech is paraphrased from the stories shared for countless generations of the "children of the large beaked bird" or *apsaalooke*.

Joe looks out the window and begins, "You are here in exactly the right place!" The audience members nod their heads in acknowledgment and agreement. Those who have ever lived in the great Little Goose Valley know this fact.

Joe describes the Crow history of the area. "The Crow Chief said, 'You have now come to my country, the Crow Country. It is a good country. The first maker, the creator of all things, has made it just right, put it in exactly the right place, and brought his favorite red children from the east and put them here." Joe clears his throat. "That is where you are now."

He continues, "About the year 1700, the Crows came and camped here. Right in this very area is where the Crow Country, a huge geographic empire started, right here. Now let me tell you about the BC days, that is Before Columbus." Joe laughs with the audience. He is a warrior capturing his audience, a soldier of words, his weapons educating us; he is an ambassador from the Crow Nation to other nations on his Mother Earth. After a long history of how the Crow tribe made it here, he ends with the following: "This is the sacred land here. The Crow chief had found the promised land. This chief took the sacred bundle with the precious grass seed and said to his people, 'We will go plant the seeds.' Lo and behold, the plants were already here. They found buffalo, deer, antelope, prairie chickens, and grouse all over."

Joe leaves us with the following advice. "The elders said to me, there are four things you must consider. My advice to you is to walk carefully. Respect your Mother Earth. It is sacred. Treat it so. Your human mothers are just a vehicle who brought you here, then went on. Treat your Mother in a respectful way and it will take care of you. Do not pollute water in any way—the streams, lakes, and rain. The air, keep it clean, even the air going into your lungs. Speak with good words. And respect fire."

Joe is the grandson of Chief Medicine Crow, White Man Runs Him (one of Gen. George Custer's scouts), and Yellowtail. He is the first historian to be featured in this book. Others will follow. Some are storytellers, some are historians and preservationists, and the rest are the history-makers of Big Horn City, Wyoming Territory.

The first white men to see the Little Goose area were trappers, outlaw gangs, soldiers, miners, and explorers. During a presentation by Elsa Spear Byron in 1981, she shared, "Captain Reynolds' expedition came through here in 1859. He wrote, 'On returning to the [wagon] train on Goose Creek, my first view of camp struck me as one of the most, of singular beauty. . . . The canvas of the painter has perpetuated few finer dreams, real or ideal.'"

Soldiers returning from Crook's Campaign and homesteaders settled the lands around Little Goose Valley. At first there were dugouts and huts that had been used by trappers, outlaw gangs, and miners. Then, in 1878, Oliver Perry (O.P.) Hanna chose a homesite on which to build what would become the first legitimate homestead in what is now Sheridan County.

The Bighorn Mountains are a well-known range in the Rocky Mountains. According to the American Association of University Women, "The name comes from Indian tribes who call it *Ahsahta*, which in English means 'the Big Horns' after the mountain sheep which were found in great numbers among the rocks and precipices of this locality." The name "Big Horn" was taken for the first town located at the foothills of the Bighorn Mountains. It is presumed that O.P. Hanna was the man who named his town Big Horn City.

Merchants, stock growers, teachers, preachers, carpenters, doctors, men, women and children, stagecoach drivers, railroad men, ranchers, cowboys, politicians, surveyors, engineers, cooks, and farmers came to live here, and the community continued to grow. In this book are the many faces of those who settled and built the town of Big Horn City.

Chapter 1 introduces the early pioneers. Chapter 2 presents images of various activities the residents performed, whether for work or pleasure. Chapter 3 features only a few of the group photographs that were found in museum files and family scrapbooks. Chapter 4, the final chapter, is an attempt to give credit to all those who have made a contribution to preserve Little Goose Valley history. The town is more commonly known now as Big Horn. If we have left out anyone, we will continue to share information, corrections, and comments in future publications, since so much has been provided for this book but, due to limited space, could not be included. Thank you and enjoy.

One

THE EARLY PIONEERS

BIG HORN CITY'S FIRST SETTLER, OLIVER PERRY HANNA. The following is from the biography of O.P. Hanna: "On August 11, 1878, with the assistance of Charlie Ferguson, I began to build the first cabin that was completed by a settler in what is now Sheridan County." (Photograph files, Wyoming–Big Horn, American Heritage Center, University of Wyoming.)

FIRST CABIN BUILT IN SHERIDAN COUNTY BY O.P. HANNA.

BIG HORN CITY'S FIRST CABIN, BUILT BY O.P. HANNA. This cabin was built about one mile south of O.P. Hanna's future Big Horn City. As written in his biography, "We cut small logs and peeled them of the bark, then we tied a rope around one end of the log and fastened the rope to the horn of the saddle and dragged them in." (1902, Glimpses of Sheridan County, WYRM.)

THE HANNA FAMILY. When it was time to settle down, O.P. Hanna chose the Little Goose Valley. In 1885, he brought his new bride, Dora Myers, to stay in his new Big Horn City hotel, the Oriental. Their three children are, from left to right, Tressie, Jess, and Laura. He is credited with a post office being established at Big Horn City and for the town being platted in 1881. (Hanna Collection, BHCHS-BTM.)

Dora Hanna and Children. Tressie, Laura, and Jess (boy on right) pose for this photograph with their mother. It appears Laura and Dora are very attentive to the boy's story, while Tressie is thoroughly bored. The family lived in Big Horn until moving to Sheridan in 1891. (Hanna Collection, BHCHS-BTM.)

Farm Equipment Used by O.P. Hanna. In February 1879, Hanna decided to take a wagon to Cheyenne, which was 350 miles away, to purchase farm equipment. As quoted in his biography, *An Old Timer's Story,* "It was [a] cold, nasty trip, with bad roads, and I had all my small team could pull. I stopped over at road houses or ranches when I could, but often I had to camp out." The equipment still stands at the site of his homestead. (JS.)

ONE OF BIG HORN CITY'S EARLIEST PIONEERS, HENRY GERDEL. In February 1879, O.P. Hanna was on his way to Cheyenne to buy farm machinery when he met Henry Gerdel and Thomas Creighton. Hanna told them of the wonderful Goose Creek country. The Gerdel and Creighton families took up ranches on Little Goose below Big Horn City. Gerdel is shown here playing a horn in the Sheridan Cornet Band, formed in 1888. (SCM.)

THE THOMAS CREIGHTON CABIN AND FIRST POST OFFICE. The mail was first delivered to the Creighton Road Ranch, located on an easy crossing of Little Goose Creek, north of what later became Big Horn City. Creighton was the first Big Horn postmaster. He later sold this ranch to Valentine Reece. (Sackett Collection, BHCHS-BTM.)

CHARLIE FARWELL. One of Big Horn City's first residents was Charlie Farwell. He operated a livery and stagecoach stop. He was born in 1850 in Wisconsin. He married Louisa Leavitt on December 17, 1884, at the Leavitt home. They were married less than two months when Louisa passed away. (Photograph files, Wyoming–Big Horn, American Heritage Center, University of Wyoming.)

FIRST BURIAL IN MOUNT HOPE CEMETERY. Louisa Farwell died on February 8, 1885. Her obituary reads, "Early Sunday morning last the sufferings of Mrs. Charles Farwell were ended and she passed into the dread and unknown beyond. We regret that our community should have suffered the loss of so estimable [a] lady, but death loves a shining mark." (JS.)

ORIENTAL HOTEL, 1883. In O.P. Hanna's biography, he states, "At that time Patrick Brothers were operating the daily stage line each way between Union Pacific Railroad and the Yellowstone. All passengers and stage men stopped at my hotel for meals. There was quite a lot of travel both ways so that the hotel was a paying investment from the first." Hanna stands at the left, nearest the horse. (BHCHS-BTM.)

BIG HORN SENTINEL ADVERTISEMENT. The one and only newspaper published in Big Horn City was the *Big Horn Sentinel*. The first edition was printed on September 13, 1884. The price was 10¢ per copy or $3.50 for a one-year subscription. It was published every Saturday morning. This issue advertised the Oriental Hotel. (*Big Horn Sentinel*, Wyoming Newspaper Project.)

MARY WILFLEY DAVIS AND HER CHILDREN. The Davises were one of the earliest families to settle in Big Horn City. William F. "Bear" Davis arrived on June 11, 1879. This photograph is of Mary Wilfley Davis with her children. Pictured are, from left to right, (first row) Mary Wilfley Davis, Elizabeth Thomas, Mary Ellen Townsend, and Amanda Jackson; (second row) Samuel Davis, Henry Davis, and William "Bear" Davis. (BHCHS-BTM.)

FRANK GROUARD. This excerpt is from an issue of the *Big Horn Pioneers*: "Frank Grouard married a squaw whose name was Suzie. She often chased Mr. Grouard with knives. (He would run to the Jackson house, in the front door, and run out the back door.) Suzie would stand in the front yard waiting for Mr. Grouard to come out the front door because she had never seen a tepee with two doors." (WYRM.)

15

BUTCH CASSIDY'S PISTOL. Zane Hilman is holding a pistol that was given to his father, Fred, in the late 1800s by a hired man working on the Hilman Ranch. Young Fred used to watch the hired man practice shooting the pistol. The true identity of the hired man was found in a note quoted in Larry Pointer's *In Search of Butch Cassidy*: "Sorry to be leaving you. The authorities are getting on to us. Best home I've ever had. Leroy Parker [Butch Cassidy]." (JS.)

RICHARD AND JENNIE PARKER. Richard and Jennie (Jeffers) Parker were originally from Clark County, Iowa. They lived there three years before moving to Wyoming in 1902. They had five children: Jim, Zelma, Dorothy, Katherine, Alma, and Joe. The Parkers ranched for more than 40 years on their property, located north of the schoolhouse. Richard served on the school board for 18 years. (Linda Davis.)

WILLIAM E. AND AMANDA DAVIS JACKSON WEDDING PHOTOGRAPH, 1867. William E. and Amanda Davis Jackson arrived in Big Horn City on August 8, 1880. The book *Big Horn Pioneers* reports, "A friend told them of a cabin which was being left vacant by the James Brothers. This cabin was located on the bank of what is now Jackson Creek." Sue Helvey Nesson, a Jackson descendant, confirmed that the famous James Gang's cabin later became the chicken coop. (BHCHS-BTM.)

GRANDMA DAVIS WITH FAMILY. Amanda Davis Jackson is at right with her mother, grandma Mary Wilfrey Davis, second from left. W.E. Jackson is in the rocking chair. Lona Martin is the young girl at left, and Durall Towns is second from the right. The Jacksons' daughter Minnie married Lemuel Martin, and their youngest daughter, Edna, married Edward Towns. (BHCHS-BTM.)

BIG HORN FOREST
RESERVE SUPERVISOR
W.E. JACKSON. On May
16, 1897, William E.
Jackson was appointed
the first supervisor of the
Big Horn Forest Reserve.
He opened his office in
a small white house near
his homestead on the
southwest corner of Big
Horn City. This house is
still standing today. His
daughter Edna Jackson
is pictured with him in
his office. He served
as the supervisor until
1910. (BHCHS-BTM.)

JANUARY 17, 1901. This
letter was sent to W.I.
Roberts of Clearmont.
It is signed, "Yours Very
Respectfully, W.E. Jackson."
The job of the first Big
Horn Forest Reserve
supervisor was not an easy
task, since most folks were
opposed to the government
imposing its authority over
ranchers. This is a reply to
a request for grazing sheep.
The letter book consists of
tissue-paper copies of the
original letters. (Schunk
Collection, BHCHS-BTM.)

WILLIAM EDWARD JACKSON. W.E. Jackson was born in 1843. His generosity included donating land and continued when he burned the brick for the Congregational church and the Wyoming Collegiate Institute. The kiln was located on Jackson Creek west of his home. Jackson served as a commissioner to organize Johnson County in 1881 and in 1888 served as commissioner for the newly formed Sheridan County. (BHCHS-BTM.)

AMANDA DAVIS JACKSON. Amanda Jackson was born in 1850 and lived most of her 82 years in the Jackson home at the southwest corner of Big Horn City. She was married to W.E. Jackson on September 15, 1867. They were one of the first families to settle in the valley. The Jacksons had three children: Charles Frank, Minnetta Hester, and Mary Edna. (BHCHS-BTM.)

JACK DOW, SURVEYOR. Born of Scottish descent in 1837 in Wisconsin, Jack Dow later graduated as a civil engineer and practiced in California, Arizona, New Mexico, and Colorado. After arriving in the northern Wyoming Territory, he surveyed and platted Big Horn City, Sheridan, and most of the county roads and ditches. (Bert Dow.)

HELEN CUTHBERTSON DOW. The obituary of Helen Cuthbertson Dow states, "Mrs. Dow had made her home at Big Horn since coming there in 1880 with her husband, a civil engineer. She was born in Scotland, April 12, 1847, and came to America with a brother in 1872, settling in Colorado." (Photograph files, Robert Helvey Collection, Wyoming–Big Horn, American Heritage Center, University of Wyoming.)

JACK DOW WITH TWO OF THE HORSES THAT BROUGHT THEM TO BIG HORN. In 1880, Jack and Helen Dow settled in the Little Goose Valley, moving from Fort Collins, Colorado. Helen drove three horses abreast, hitched to a light wagon containing their household goods and a year's supply of food. This photograph is supposedly two of the three horses. (Bert Dow.)

THE JACK DOW FAMILY, C. 1900. Along with raising their nieces and nephews—children of Helen's sister Janet Lothian of Buffalo—Jack and Helen Dow also adopted Benitta. She was born in Colorado, and Helen brought her as an infant to Big Horn City. Pictured are, from left to right, Mary, Bert, Benitta, Helen, and Jack. (BHCHS-BTM.)

JACK AND "AUNTIE" HELEN DOW.
Helen Dow was childless, so when her sister passed away, she and her husband reared her nieces and nephew, hence the reason she was known as "Auntie Dow." They filed on a section of land that they made into a horticultural showplace. The Dows were the first to successfully plant an orchard of apples, cherries, pears, and plums. (Bert Dow.)

JACK DOW'S GRANDSON JACK USING THE LEVEL. This instrument was used by pioneer Jack Dow when surveying ditches, roads, towns, and homesteads in northern Wyoming. Jack, shown here, was the son of Cuthbertson "Bert" Lothian Dow, who was the nephew of Jack and Helen Dow. (Bert Dow.)

JOHN HENRY SACKETT. John Sackett arrived in Big Horn City on October 12, 1880, with his partner Charles W. Skinner. They were merchants, freighters, and ranchers. He married Martha Burd on March 17, 1871. John was the postmaster for Big Horn City from 1881 to 1885. The 1885–1887 Johnson County Fairs were held on his land. On April 2, 1888, he sold his interest in the Big Horn Mercantile to C.W. Skinner. (BHCHS-BTM.)

MARTHA ANN BURD SACKETT. Martha Ann Burd Sackett was born on April 1, 1851. She and John had seven children, Lee, Carl, Ursula, Clyde, Hugh, Ross, and a son who died at birth. Carl served as a US district attorney in Wyoming. Ursula married James Gatchell, the well-known collector of Indian and Western artifacts. Later, the Jim Gatchell Museum was built to house his precious collection. (Chuck Custis and John Custis.)

23

SACKETT AND SKINNER'S FREIGHT WAGON, OCTOBER 12, 1880. John Sackett and Charles W. Skinner hauled four freight wagons from Cheyenne. Skinner drove his own 10-mule team, pulling two wagons, riding the left wheel-mule with a single rein held in his hand attached to the bridle bit of the left lead-mule. A rope from the brake poles on the left side of each wagon was tied to his saddle horn. (George Harper and family in honor of Charles Skinner's granddaughter Mary.)

BIG HORN MERCANTILE, MARCH 1884. Big Horn Mercantile was the first mercantile established in what is now Sheridan County. Pictured are, from left to right, O.P. Benefield, John W. Austin, William E. Jackson, Charles Farwell, Carl Sackett, John H. Sackett (left in doorway), Charles W. Skinner, two unidentified, Oliver P. Hanna, two Wolfe boys, J.W. Wolfe, and an unidentified man on a horse. The child in the window is a Sackett boy. (George Harper and family in honor of Charles Skinner's granddaughter Mary.)

MARY AND CHARLES W. SKINNER'S WEDDING PHOTOGRAPH, JUNE 7, 1885. Mary Alice Hayes was born in Missouri and later moved to Custer Station, Montana, where she met her future husband, Charles William Skinner. He had been hauling freight to and from Big Horn City to Custer Station once the railroad had been built across southern Montana. (George Harper and family in honor of Charles Skinner's granddaughter Mary.)

CHARLES AND MARY SKINNER'S WEDDING CERTIFICATE. On June 7, 1885, Charles William Skinner and Mary Alice Hayes were married in Big Horn City. The minister of the gospel was George W. Benton, who officiated the marriage in the "County of Johnson, and Territory of Wyoming." Witnesses for the couple were Hallie Coffeen and T.J. Green. Charles was 29 and Mary was only 19. (George Harper and family in honor of Charles Skinner's granddaughter Mary.)

Christmas Eve Ball.

Yourself and ladies are respectfully invited to attend a Christmas Ball, to be given

AT

Sackett & Skinner's Hall,

Big Horn City, Dec. 24, 1882.

Music by the Big Horn City Band.——Tickets, including supper, $5,00.

CHRISTMAS EVE BALL. This gold, gilt-edged invitation reads, "Yourself and ladies are respectfully invited to attend a Christmas Ball, to be given—at Sackett and Skinner's Hall—Big Horn City, Dec. 24, 1882. Music by the Big Horn City Band—Tickets, including supper, $5.00." (George Harper and family in honor of Charles Skinner's granddaughter Mary.)

CHARLES W. SKINNER FAMILY. Charles and Mary pose with their four children. From left to right are Fred, Mary (seated), Maud, Nellie, Charles, and Jack. Maud married Herman Langheldt, and they had one daughter, Mary. The Big Horn Mercantile, now known as "the Merc," has been cared for by the descendants of Charles Skinner. (George Harper and family in honor of Charles Skinner's granddaughter Mary.)

Big Horn P.O. January 8th 1881
Minutes of a Meeting held at
the above place to Organize a Town
To be known as the Big Horn City
The Said Town or City to be located
at or within one Mile of the present
Site of the Big Horn P.O.
Meeting Called to Order
and [name] Chosen Chairman
and C.P. [name] Secretary.

JANUARY 8, 1881. These are the minutes of the first stockholders' meeting of Big Horn City Company, Carbon County, Wyoming Territory. It was held at the Big Horn Post Office. The document states, "Minutes of a meeting held at the above place to organize a Town to be known as Big Horn City. The said Town or City to be located at or within one mile of the present site of the Big Horn P.O." (DH Vol. 2 and BHCHS-BTM.)

COLD SPRING SEED FARM. This is the cover of the Cold Spring Seed Farm catalogue. Gabriel J. Lambrigger homesteaded along Jackson Creek. As published on February 28, 1889, in the *Sheridan Post*: "G.J. Lambrigger, Sheridan county's Nurseryman and Seed Dealer of Big Horn, Wyo., wishes to announce to the public that his Nursery and Seed catalogues are now ready for distribution." The catalogue had a red cover and 48 pages. (BHCHS-BTM.)

FIRST ANNUAL CATALOGUE
—of—
Seeds, Plants and Fruits,
—FROM—

1889.

COLD SPRING SEED FARM,
BIG HORN CITY,
SHERIDAN COUNTY, - WYOMING
GABRIEL J. LAMBRIGGER, Proprietor.

—OFFICE OF—

COLD SPRING SEED FARM,

G. J. Lambrigger, Proprietor.

Big Horn City, Sheridan Co. Wyo.

_____ 188

Mrs Lambrigger and daughters

G.J. LAMBRIGGER, PROPRIETOR. This piece of stationery was found with the following photograph. It reads: "Office of—COLD SPRING SEED FARM—G. J. Lambrigger, Proprietor. Big Horn City, Sheridan Co, Wyo., 188-." The seed farm later became the site of Jerome Brown's cheese factory. The Lambrigger family moved to Knox County, Nebraska. (BHCHS-BTM.)

LIZZIE AND DAUGHTERS. The date of this photograph and the names of Lizzie and G.J. Lambrigger's children are unknown. The Lambrigger home later became the home of the Jerome Brown, Gus Olson, and Emil Benson families. Gabriel was the brother of Alfonse, Alfred, and Leo Lambrigger. The Lambrigger brothers were original Big Horn City stockholders. (BHCHS-BTM.)

DAN HILMAN ON OLD RED. Dan Hilman was born in Maryland and was the brother of Jennie Hilman Davis, wife of William "Bear" Davis. He arrived in the Little Goose Valley on May 31, 1881. He married Mary Lydia Davis, daughter of William "Bear" Davis, on February 4, 1883. (Hilman family.)

BAR ELEVEN HILMAN DUDE RANCH. The following is from an interview with Fred Hilman in the *Big Horn Pioneers* book, published in 1961: "Dude ranching in Wyoming became a reality in the summer of 1889 when father and mother Hilman first took and cared for two paying guests who came from Ames, Iowa. Their names were Mrs. Virginia Allen and Mrs. Linsey. Their husbands owned and operated vast ranches in the Sand Hills of Nebraska." (Hilman family.)

EDITH GERDEL KNODLE AND FRED HILMAN. Big Horn City's first white child, Edith Gerdel Knodle, born in 1880, and the first white boy, Fred Hilman, born in 1884, help celebrate the Diamond Jubilee of Sheridan County in 1963. They were born to early Big Horn City pioneers in what later became Sheridan County. Edith's parents were Peter and Theresa Gerdel, and Fred's parents were Dan and Lydia Hilman. (WYRM.)

THE ABRAHAM ZULLIG FAMILY C. 1900. Abraham Zullig was born in Arbon, Switzerland, on April 15, 1834. He later immigrated to the United States and settled in Missouri. He married Elizabeth Sharen. They came by covered wagon via Cheyenne, arriving in Big Horn City on August 6, 1882. Pictured are, from left to right, (first row) Abraham, Archibald, and Elizabeth Zullig; (second row) Conrad, William, Nathaniel Croghan (son-in-law), Susan Zullig Croghan, and Herbert. (John Zullig.)

BILLY MANN. One of the best jockeys and horse trainers in the Big Horn area was Billy Mann. His jockey outfit and boots are on display at the Bozeman Trail Museum. (BHCHS-BTM)

CONRAD ZULLIG, WORLD WAR I. Conrad Zullig was born May 3, 1887, to Abraham and Elizabeth Zullig. He was their fifth child. Conrad married Leona Jenkins and bought a ranch east of the Zullig homestead. He passed away at the Soldiers and Sailors Home in Buffalo, Wyoming, on June 22, 1981. (Zullig family.)

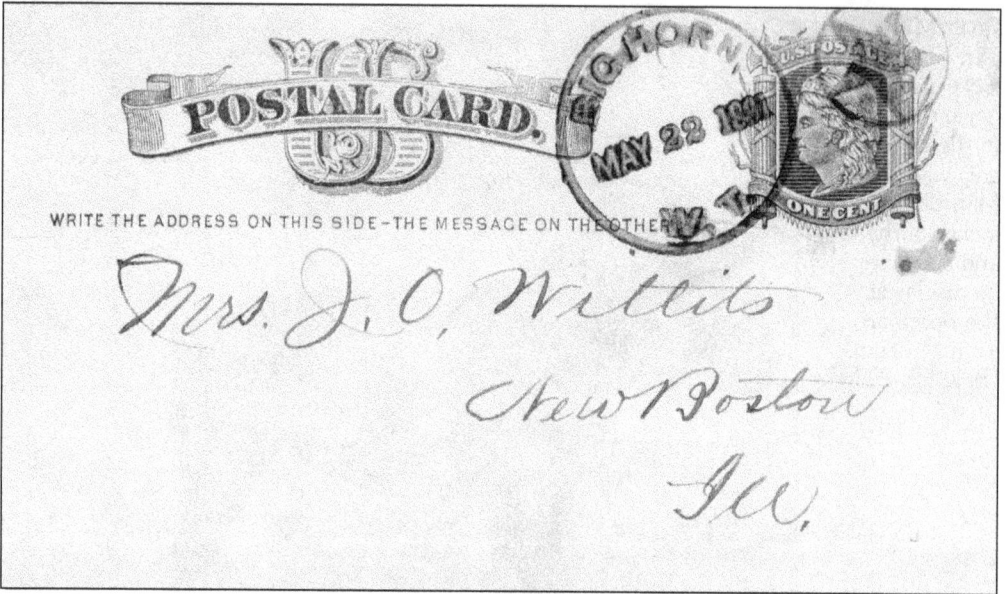

POSTCARD MAILED IN BIG HORN CITY, 1881. In the spring of 1881, James Orr Willits was searching for a new place to live. He started in Colorado and rode a saddle horse across Wyoming and into Montana. On his way back home to Illinois, he stopped in Big Horn City and sent this postcard, dated May 22, 1881, to his wife, Hattie. The back of this card is on the following page. (Victor Garber family.)

JAMES ORR WILLITS. J.O. Willits was raised in New Boston, Illinois, worked with the family cattle-feeding business, traveled west with a wagon train, and worked for Wells Fargo in California. His trip home involved sailing down the West Coast, walking across the Isthmus of Panama, and sailing to New York before returning to New Boston. He married Hattie Clark on July 21, 1870. (Victor Garber family.)

Big Horn Sund, May 22 ᵈ '81

Mrs Willits I am well & will start home from here in day or two hope to get home by next Sunday

Yours

JO Willits

POSTCARD MAILED IN BIG HORN CITY, 1881. "Mrs. Willits, I am well & will start home from here in day or two. Hope to get home by next Sunday. Yours, JO Willits." This may be the earliest known piece of mail that the Bozeman Trail Museum has seen, even though the post office had been established in 1879. (Victor Garber family.)

HATTIE CLARK WILLITS. Hattie was born in New York and raised in Mount Pleasant, Iowa. She graduated from Iowa Wesleyan College in 1869. She and J.O. had two children, Paul and Nellie, prior to moving West. Two more children were born in Big Horn City: Areli, who died at age 10, and Vie, who lived to be 101, passing in 1985. (Victor Garber family.)

ALVIN LAROY GARBER. "Roy" was born in Missouri on December 30, 1879. He came west to work as a camp tender for a large sheep operation in the Broadus, Montana, area. Then he worked for the Beckton Stock Farm sheep operation and later as a general ranch hand for the Moncreiffe Ranch. He married Vie Willits on July 18, 1911. (Victor Garber family.)

VIE WILLITS GARBER. Vie was born on July 18, 1884, to J.O. and Hattie Willits. Vie's major master's thesis in botany was written in 1911 and was titled "The Vascular Plants of the Little Goose Water-shed." Her minor thesis was titled "The Bozeman Trail." She rode horseback from Fort Reno to Fort Custer studying the flora along the Bozeman Trail. (Victor Garber family.)

VIE AND ALVIN LAROY GARBER.
After their marriage, Roy and Vie
managed the ranch properties for
the Willits. They built a small
cabin next to the Willits' stone
house, where Orr and Victor
were born. A larger home was
built in 1924 when Eugene was
born. (Victor Garber family.)

MAKINLEY GUY WOOD FAMILY.
This photograph was probably
taken in 1901. Pictured are,
from left to right, Guy holding
Iris, Beth, and "Chip" sitting on
Nellie's lap. Nellie passed away
on August 11, 1903, leaving
the three young children to be
raised by her parents, J.O. and
Hattie Willits. Guy trained
polo ponies for Malcolm
Moncreiffe, and the young
family lived on the Moncreiffe
ranch. (Victor Garber family.)

DAVID AND MAGDELENA GARBER. The parents of Alvin Laroy "Roy" Garber came to Big Horn in 1919. They lived with Roy and his wife, Vie. David and Magdelena were married in 1859. They had 11 children. David passed away in 1925, just two months prior to the couple's 66th wedding anniversary. (Victor Garber family.)

LETTER TO HANNAH TORREY. The letter from George Washington Benton to his future bride, Helen, reads, "Oxford December 3rd, 1849—Dearest, According to my promise and with much pleasure I embrace this early opportunity to write you. I have your picture before me, and the privilege of using the pen and paper as a medium of communion with you, but gladly would I exchange them for a personal interview with you. . . . I arrived home safe about 1/2 past 8." (Elsa Spear Byron Collection at WYRM.)

REV. GEORGE WASHINGTON AND HANNAH TORREY BENTON. The Benton family arrived in Big Horn City on September 14, 1881. Elder Benton was a descendant of Roger Williams, who arrived on the *Mayflower*. As a Baptist minister and trained homeopathic doctor, Benton became a welcomed settler in the area. He performed weddings, funerals, and Sunday services along with pulling teeth, setting broken bones, and assisting with births. (Elsa Spear Byron Collection at WYRM.)

HANS KLEIBER'S SKETCH OF BIG HORN CITY. Hans Kleiber came West to work in the lumber camps and spent several years working for the forest service. He learned to appreciate the Western scenes and began to paint. Later, he tried the etching trade and became known as "Etcher Laureate of the Rockies." This scene is titled *Leaving the Frontier* and depicts Big Horn City in the late 1800s. (BHCHS-BTM.)

ROY BENTON ON FAT DUKE. His obituary states, "He raised Hereford cattle and 39 times his animals topped the Omaha grass fed cattle market." Roy was the son of John and Martha Benton. He was only three when his family moved to Wyoming. He lived his entire life on the family ranch. Roy served on the Big Horn school board several terms yet had no children and never married. (BHCHS-BTM.)

VIRGINIA BELLE BENTON SPEAR 1887 DIARY. This rare diary was found in the Elsa Spear Byron Collection. The Spear family diaries are rich in other family histories. On these two pages, Virginia mentions her father taking meat to Mr. Rose, her brother-in-law Doc, her stepbrother Kinney, the Hanna home, and that Monday the 14th being the fourth anniversary of Dan Hilman and Lida [sic] Davis's wedding. (Elsa Spear Byron collection at WYRM.)

ROCK CREEK STAGE LINE BLACKSMITH SHOP AND BARN. The Rock Creek Stage Line came through Big Horn City along the Bozeman Trail. The blacksmith shop was used for several years by different owners. Today it serves as the Big Horn City Historical Society's museum, more commonly called the Bozeman Trail Museum. The barn was also used for several years but eventually was torn down in the mid-1900s. (BHCHS-BTM.)

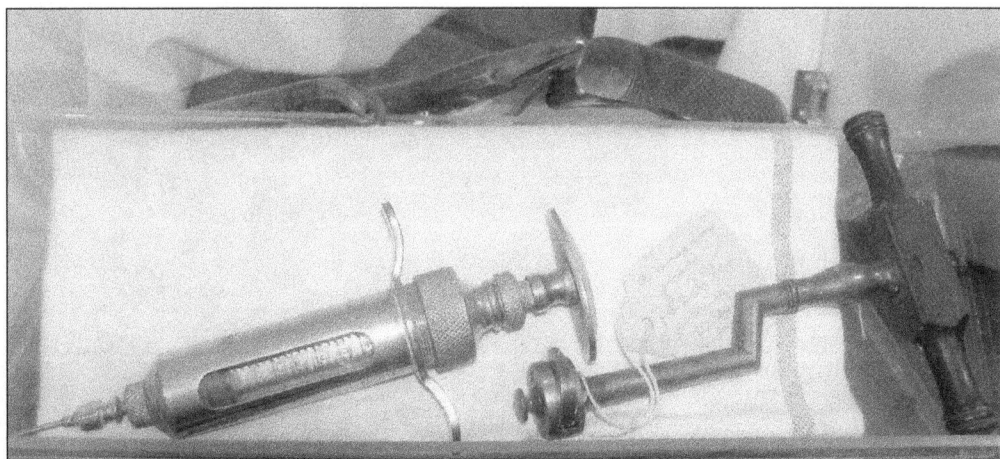

REV. GEORGE WASHINGTON BENTON'S DENTAL TOOLS. Rev. G.W. Benton's dental tools are ominous yet provided the pioneers with relief. His tools were carried in a large black case. The interior was made with several compartments and trays. The exterior was covered with black leather. Upon returning home during a blizzard, he contracted pneumonia and died on February 4, 1895. These dental tools have been gifted to the Bozeman Trail Museum. (BHCHS-BTM.)

WILL SKINNER FAMILY. In 1881, Will came to Big Horn to work for his brother Charles in the Big Horn Mercantile. He married Josephine Barnett on June 6, 1886, in Bentonville, Johnson County, Wyoming. Emma was their oldest child, at left, and Robert was their youngest, at right. Will was bucked off a horse in 1895. He became deaf and blind from this accident. He died on December 11, 1904. (BHCHS-BTM.)

JO SKINNER. Josephine stands with her sister seated at right. Jo was known to Big Horn residents as "Aunt Jo." She had come to the Little Goose Valley in 1885 by covered wagon. She later returned to Big Horn after her husband, Will, died. She managed the Oriental Hotel for several years. Her obituary states that she passed away September 4, 1937, "of a slight stroke and a heart attack." (BHCHS-BTM.)

GEORGE SKINNER. In 1890, George Skinner
came to Big Horn City to work in his
brother's store, the Big Horn Mercantile.
He served as a sergeant in Troop E in the
Spanish-American War in 1898. He served
under Col. Jay L. Torrey. They were more
commonly called "Torrey's Rough Riders."
In May 1899, he married Osa Maude Reed.
They later purchased the Samuel Jennings
homestead on Kruse Creek. (BHCHS-BTM.)

OSA MAUDE REED SKINNER. Maude Reed
was born on September 6, 1879. Her
family later moved in a covered wagon
to the Big Horn area to the Val Reece
ranch. She was wed to George Skinner
in May 1899. Maude and George had
three children, Gouverneur, Lorraine,
and Kathleen. They lived and worked in
the Big Horn area until 1942, when they
moved to Oregon. (BHCHS-BTM.)

MINNIE REECE CUSTIS IN LARGE BLACK HAT, C. 1900. The Custis family is not able to identify the lady and gentleman on the left, but Minnie Reece Custis is on the right. They could possibly be a younger brother and sister of Minnie's. This "cabinet portrait" photograph was taken in Big Horn, Wyoming, at the Chancy Haven and Co. (Chuck Custis and John Custis.)

JOHN AND MINNIE REECE CUSTIS. This photograph was taken in Eugene, Oregon. John was mining in Oregon for approximately two years and then returned to Big Horn. He was an original lot owner in Big Horn City, owning Block 10, Lots 14 and 16. He also homesteaded south of Big Horn. He first arrived here in April 1882. (Georgia Torland.)

John Custis's Rattlesnake Jack Mine. John Custis was one of the first pioneers to bring livestock to this area and continued to ranch, since gold mining was not profitable. This is the Notice of Location filing claim for the Rattlesnake Jack Mine, discovered on July 18, 1898. It was located on the west side of Big Goose Creek about one mile, "so staked by W.T. Barrow and J.W. Custis." (Chuck Custis and John Custis.)

NOTICE OF LOCATION.

TO ALL WHOM IT MAY CONCERN:

Notice is hereby given that the undersigned, having complied with the requirements of Chapter VI of Title 33 of the Revised Statutes of the United State, and the local mining laws, rules and regulations, have located The Rattle sanake Jack

situated in _____ Mining District, County of Johnson and State of Wyoming and described as follows Situated on the west side of Big Goose about one mile. one claim 750 feet in a northerly and 750 feet in a Southerly direction from center Stake also 300 to guyck side of center stake making is final feet on this Load we claim all Dips Spurs angles and veriations within these Boundarys

_____ Located by _____ Locator.
W.T. Barrow Locator.
J.W. Custis Locator.
_____ Locator.
Discovered July 18 1898 By _____ Agent.
Located Aug 24 1899 Attest

Charles W. and Minerva Goodrich Bard on Their Wedding Day, 1877. Charlie and Minerva first homesteaded near Cheyenne. He had worked as a buffalo hunter and roundup cook. They sold out in 1882; loaded two covered wagons with household goods, a hay mowing machine, and a small hay rake; and set out for northern Wyoming Territory. This trip took one month before they settled near Meade Creek. (Paddy Bard.)

CHARLES BARD AND HIS BARREL OF SPICES. Charles had learned to be a cook on early roundups in Colorado. He loved to cook, as shown in this photograph taken in Canon City, Colorado. This barrel of spices has printed on the side "Complete—Flour Chest" with the five drawers labeled Soda, Nutmeg, Cinnamon, Spice, and Pepper. (Paddy Bard.)

TODE AND FLOYD BARD. Ten-year-old Floyd, right, and nine-year-old Charles "Tode" Bard were full-fledged horse wranglers at a young age. Tode later rode in Buffalo Bill's Wild West Show. Soon after this photograph was taken, Floyd was in Buffalo the day the invaders of the Johnson County Cattle War were escorted to town by the US Cavalry. (*Horse Wrangler* by Floyd Bard.)

MABEL SUMNER BARD. Mabel's parents died when she was a young girl of seven. She lived with her brother for a while, then moved to Wyoming to live with her sister. She married Floyd Bard on December 2, 1902. They lived in the Big Horn area for more than 60 years. She was a member of the Rebekah Lodge of Big Horn. (BHCHS-BTM.)

CHARLES BARD'S HOTEL REGISTER, 1894. Charles ran several different eating establishments and hotels in the late 1800s. These are F.A. Myers's boarding charges for "self and wife" and payments made from February 2 through May 1. The total bill was $119.60 paid with cash and bartered items: 50 pounds of flour for $2; wood $2.25; 2,000 pounds of potatoes for $20; fruit trees totaling $55; and other trees for $6.35. (Paddy Bard.)

45

SACKETT & SKINNER,

Wholesale and Retail Dealers in

GENERAL ⊕ MERCHANDISE.

BIG HORN, WYOMING.

OUR DRY GOODS !

Stock consists of the fullest line ever shipped to this county, to which is now being added an extra line of

FALL AND WINTER GOODS.

In Groceries we have recently received a fresh supply which we selected from the largest wholesale houses in the East, hence we don't intend to be undersold by any house in this section.

IN BOOTS⊕SHOES

HATS, CAPS, AND

CLOTHING,

We have an endless variety. A complete stock

Heavy and Shelf Hardware

PAINTS, OILS, &C.

150,000 Feet of

NATIVE + LUMBER !

At lower cash figures than elsewhere in this county. Also an unlimited supply of LATHS and SHINGLES.

BIG HORN SENTINEL. This advertisement was found in the *Big Horn Sentinel*. The newspaper was printed in a shop just south of the Oriental Hotel. It was published from September 13, 1884, until October 19, 1889. Harry E. Becker was the editor. This advertisement featured the Sackett and Skinner store, the Big Horn Mercantile, which is still owned by the descendants of Charlie Skinner. (Wyoming Newspaper Project.)

TOM TYNAN. As a young man, Tom Tynan worked as a bookkeeper for the Big Horn Mercantile. He was trained as a boxer, and he and Robert Long had boxing matches. He also was good at math and performed mental arithmetic, which he taught to young boys. He married Vinnie Bean of Beckton and later served as the state superintendent of public instruction. (WYRM.)

SKINNER FAMILY OF CLARKSVILLE, IOWA. Robert and Mary Hickman Skinner had 10 children. Pictured are, from left to right, (first row) Mary Hickman Skinner, Hugh Ellsworth, Charles William (who came to Big Horn City in 1880 and established a grocery/dry goods business), May Eleanor, and Robert; (second row) Washington George, Edgar Thomas, Robert John, Eugene Francis, Franklin Benjamin, Henry James, and William Mathew. Charles, George, and William were early pioneers in Big Horn City. (BHCHS-BTM.)

JANE AND WILLYS BRADFORD SPEAR. On October 17, 1853, Willys Bradford Spear married Jane Ferguson Wood. She had two children from a previous marriage, Makinley and Lorrinda. Willys and Jane had eight children: Ocianna, Mary, John, Charles, Hulett ("Doc"), Willis, Emily, and Annie. They came to Big Horn City in 1883. He was known as "Willys with a 'y'." His signature confirms this spelling. (Elsa Spear Byron Collection at WYRM.)

47

VIRGINIA BELLE BENTON SPEAR. In 1881, the Benton family arrived in Big Horn. The following was written in Virginia's diary: "September 14th: we left Shell Creek and ate our dinner near Mr. Terrill's ranch where Mr. Wright is living. Came by way of Meade's cutoff to Little Goose Creek and saw our new home in all the glory of autumn tints in the leaves of the wild plum and chokecherries, cottonwood, quaking asp, birch and willow." (Elsa Spear Byron Collection at WYRM.)

WILLIS MOSES SPEAR. Willis Moses Spear married Virginia Belle Benton on November 18, 1885, at the Benton home. Virginia's father was the Reverend George W. Benton, who performed the ceremony. Willis was a rancher, farmer, dude rancher, county commissioner, and state senator from Sheridan County. He served in the state legislature from 1918 to 1932. He and Virginia had four children: Jessamine, Willis Jr., Phil, and Elsa. (Elsa Spear Byron Collection at WYRM.)

ELSA SPEAR'S 1911 DIARY. An excerpt from her diary reads, "A pack trip to climb Cloud Peak. July 2—Sunday—Lake Geneva . . . Bill Gollings cut E's and My pictures. Laid around and read for awhile. Jr. came up then and had left Happy Jack Hobbled on the West side made 34 in party and 57 horses." Per Elsa's captions, at center left is camp artist Bill Gollings, and at lower left is Lake Geneva looking south. (Elsa Spear Byron Collection at WYRM.)

MAKINLEY WOOD FAMILY. Makinley and Mary Wood had nine children. They had lost three children before this photograph was taken. Pictured are, from left to right, (first row) Clyde Rex, Makinley, and Mary with Robert Otto in front; (second row) Makinley Guy, Paul Ray, Harry Roy, and Frank Egbert. They arrived in Big Horn City on September 25, 1883. (Marce Lee Nelson.)

LORRINDA JANE WOOD SCHNEIDER. Makinley Wood was the older brother to Lorrinda. She moved to the Little Goose Valley in 1893 after the death of her husband, Christopher Schneider, who passed in 1891. They had nine children. Most of the children moved here with their mother. (Marce Lee Nelson.)

HATTIE WILLITS AND GRANDCHILDREN, 1905. Hattie and J.O. Willits raised three grandchildren born to their daughter Nellie Willits Wood: Beth, at left, born in 1888; Iris, born in 1900; and "Chip," born in 1901, in front. Nellie passed away on August 11, 1903, at Dr. John Kellogg's sanitarium in Battle Creek, Michigan. Hattie was 50 and J.O. was 55 at the time of Nellie's passing. Iris lived to be 100 years old. (Victor Garber family.)

50TH WEDDING ANNIVERSARY, OCTOBER 17, 1903. Willys and Jane Ferguson Spear celebrated their 50th wedding anniversary in Billings, Montana, with their entire family. (Marilyn Bilyeu and Elsa Spear Byron Collection at WYRM.)

J.O. AND HATTIE WILLITS. J.O. and Hattie are pictured with their grandchildren on the porch of their stone house in 1921. Pictured are, from left to right, Chip Wood, Orr Garber, Victor on Hattie's lap, Beth, J.O., and Iris Wood. The stone house has been in the Willits family since 1901. Victor's son Roy now owns the house. The land has been in the family since the spring of 1881. (Victor Garber family.)

EDNA BROWN AND PAUL RAY WOOD ON THEIR WEDDING DAY. The couple was married on October 28, 1897, in Big Horn City. Paul was a rancher and carpenter. He had played polo on the early Moncreiffe Ranch teams. They had six children. Edna's father, Jerome, was a county commissioner during the Johnson County Cattle War. Her diary contains firsthand information surrounding that historic event. (Marce Lee Nelson.)

VIRGINIA BELLE BENTON SPEAR WITH HER TWO OLDEST CHILDREN. This photograph was taken on June 5, 1889. The following was written on the back of the photograph: "Virginia Belle Benton Spear & Jessa & Jr. Belle Spear 25 years 6 months. Jessa Spear 2 years 9 months, Willis Benton Spear 1 year 5 months. Goff Photo." Willis was more commonly known as "Junior." Sylvia Jessamine was born on September 11, 1886, and Willis Benton was born on January 7, 1888. (Elsa Spear Byron Collection at WYRM.)

DEAR EDNA. This page, from an autograph book belonging to Edna Brown, was dated December 31, 1890 AD. It reads, "Dear Edna: Not like the rose may our friendship wither; But like the evergreen, live forever. From your true friend, Alvah S. Hopkins." This was written when the Brown family lived near Buffalo. Edna was 15 in 1890. (Marce Lee Nelson.)

THE BENTON FAMILY HOME. This home was built by the Benton family. The home belonged to John and Martha Benton. It later became the home of their son Roy. After Roy's death, the home was purchased by David and Judy Garber. They have preserved the home's historic character. (*The Benton Home*, by Jessamine Spear Johnson, used by permission of the Johnson family and X4, LLC. © 2011, X4, LLC, all rights reserved.)

HENRY ASA COFFEEN. He was one of Sheridan County's most industrious pioneers. Born in 1841 in Ohio and highly involved with public speaking, publishing, singing, teaching, and traveling, Henry settled in Big Horn City in 1884. Later he relocated his store to Main Street in Sheridan. One of the busiest streets in the state of Wyoming is named in his honor: Coffeen Avenue. (CHIEF, INC.)

SHERIDAN STAMPEDE, JULY 4, 1914. This postcard's photograph is called "Bulldogging Steer from Auto" and was taken by Alex Serdel. The postcard was printed by the Coffeen family and sold in their stores. Henry's son Herbert became a leading businessman in Sheridan plus a wonderful friend to the Indian tribes. One of his most beloved endeavors was his store and trading post, named the Sign of the Teepee. (CHIEF, INC.)

Bulldogging Steer from Auto, by Alex. Serdel.

Sheridan Stampede July 4. 1914.

HENRY ASA COFFEEN INVOICE. The invoice states, "H.A. COFFEEN—DEALER IN—GENERAL MERCHANDISE—Big Horn City, 188_, Wyoming Ter." It is addressed to "Messrs. Sackett & Skinner for items such as nails, sugar, stove polish in exchange for lumber and oats." The total amount of items exchanged was $454.95. The bill began September 22, 1884, and was settled on November 25, 1884. (George Harper and family in honor of Charles Skinner's granddaughter Mary.)

BIG HORN STILL AHEAD. An advertisement in this issue of the *Big Horn Sentinel* reads, "H.A. Coffeen's Store Leads in Reductions. The Days of Monopoly Stores are Ended In Johnson County. Read Our Prices and Pull for Big Horn. Not Alone in Groceries, but in Clothing, Dry Goods, Hardware, And Notions. We are Determined to Keep Ahead. We sell for Cash or equivalent." (*Big Horn Sentinel*, Wyoming Newspaper Project.)

THE WOOD BROTHERS. Written on the back of this photograph is, "Standing left to right: Frank (17 years, ten months), Harry Wood (20 years, three months). Seated left to right: Ray (22 years, 2 months) and Guy Wood (24 years, 1 month). Probably taken in 1896." (Marce Lee Nelson.)

1888 WEDDING PHOTOGRAPH OF LEMUEL E. MARTIN AND MINNETTA H. JACKSON. Lemuel was the superintendent for the Colorado Colony Ditch Company. Minnie (Minnetta) had been the superintendent at the Wyoming Girls' School for 24 years, retiring in 1949. The Reed residence, which was purchased by the state for the Wyoming Girls' School, had once belonged to Verner Reed, who was associated with the Colorado Colony Land Company. (BHCHS-BTM.)

COLORADO COLONY DITCH COMPANY.
The first entry in the accounting
records is April 6, 1886. Some of the
items listed are cook stove fixtures for
$27.35; three shovels for $4.50; six and
a half pounds of coffee for $1.65; and a
load of straw for 50¢. It appears Lemuel
Martin, who was superintendent of the
company, had not paid himself wages
for 16 months, claiming, "L.E. Martin
to 16 mos. labor from June 29, 1884 to
Jan. 1886. $1,200.00." The last entry
stated is for 500 pounds of hay for $5.
(Schunk Collection, BHCHS-BTM.)

LEMUEL MARTIN AND CREW. This group
of men and mules was the industrious
Colorado Colony Ditch crew that came
to the Little Goose Valley in 1884 from
Boulder, Colorado. This photograph
was taken in Cheyenne, Wyoming,
in July 1884 on their way to Big Horn
City, Wyoming Territory. Written
on the back is, "Papa Martin and his
crew." The crew was outfitted with
mule teams and five prairie schooners.
(Helvey Collection, BHCHS-BTM.)

THE MARTINS. This photograph was taken before Lemuel and Minnie Martin's son, Edward, went to serve in World War I. They also had a daughter, Lona, who later became Mrs. Robert T. Helvey. In a footnote found in the book *Big Horn Pioneers*, Carl Sackett mentions, "Mr. Martin was a very courteous and considerate gentleman. He was a good singer and played the organ well, helping in entertainments." (Helvey Collection, BHCHS-BTM.)

1885 HOLT'S NEW MAP OF WYOMING. Big Horn City is listed along with "L. Goose Cr." (Little Goose Creek) on this area map. The only two pioneer homesteads identified are Davis and Skinner. Another ranch listed is the Hepps' near Fort Phil Kearney. The Hepp family later had three daughters who came to Big Horn to live. (David Rumsey Map Collection website.)

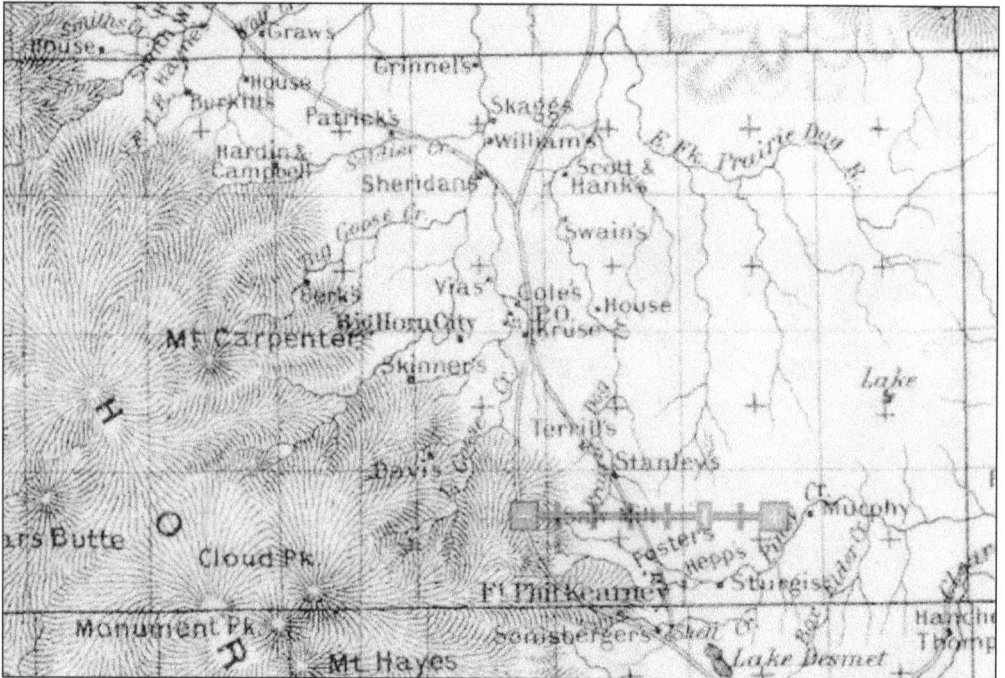

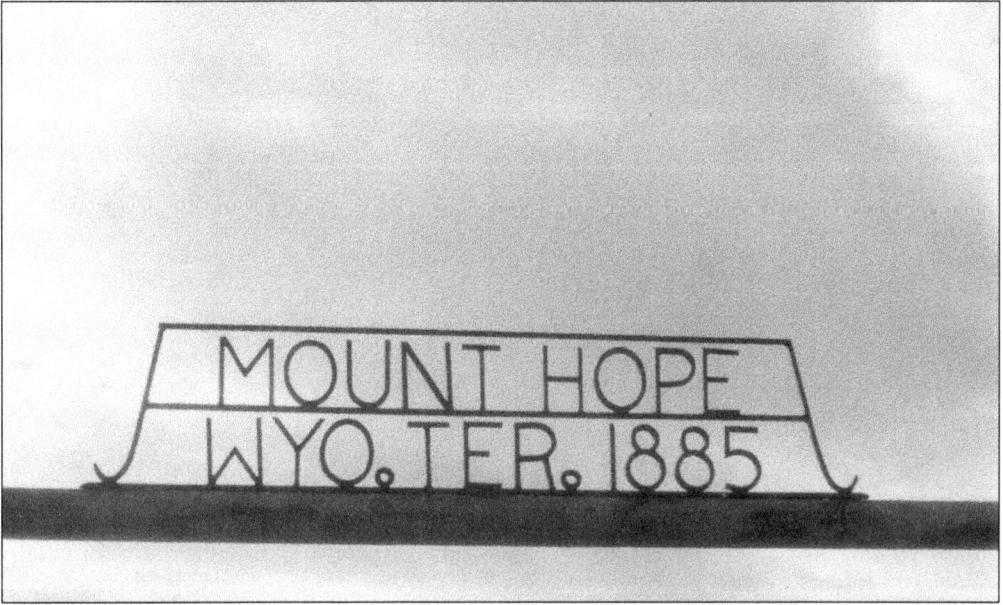

MOUNT HOPE CEMETERY, WYOMING TERRITORY, 1885. On Wednesday, February 5, 1885, it was decided that the little town of Big Horn City needed a cemetery. "On motion of H.A. Coffeen the meeting proceeded [to] organize a cemetery company. . . . The name Mount Hope was chosen as name of cemetery and company." The first burial took place on the following Tuesday, February 11. Louise Farwell's obituary stated, "Death of an Estimable Lady but death loves a shining mark." (JS.)

MERRITT DANA HOUGHTON, 1884. M.D. Houghton was a famous muralist drawing Wyoming towns in the 1900s. This photograph was taken on the Christian J. Hepp ranch, showing three bull teams hauling two wagons each up the hill near Pilot Knob (to the left) south of Fort Phil Kearney, facing towards mountains. His original signature is on the back: "Photographed May 1884 By M.D. Houghton." This original photograph is owned by Gary McCoy. (Gary McCoy.)

Rosa Hepp On Her Way to Teach School. Written on the back of this photograph is "Teaching on Little Piney." Rosa most likely lived at home with her parents during the years she taught school. Her parents' ranch was located near Fort Phil Kearney. Rosa married Gus Olson on April 26, 1913. The couple then moved to Big Horn and lived west of town on the old Lambrigger place. (Inga McCoy.)

Hepp Family, c. 1905. Christian J. and Rosa Weller Hepp pose with their six children while living on their homestead on Piney Creek. Christian was more commonly knows as "C.J." Pictured are, from left to right, Elsie, Karl (on C.J.'s lap), Rosa (the eldest daughter), Harry (on Rosa's lap), Lora, and Clara. In 1888, they had lost a daughter, Erlis, who is buried in the Fort Phil Kearney cemetery. (Gary McCoy.)

GOING TO A FUNERAL. Some Christian J. Hepp family members refer to this photograph as going to the funeral of young, Harry Hepp who died in 1910 of appendicitis. Pictured are, from left to right, Karl, Elsie, Rosa, Clara, Lora, and mother Rosa Hepp. Three of the girls later became residents of Big Horn: Rosa married Gus Olson, Lora married Emil Benson, and Clara married Tom White. (Gary McCoy.)

LOOKING WEST ON FIRST STREET. The photographer was standing next to the Big Horn Mercantile when this was taken. The brick First Congregational Church was built in 1893 along with the Wyoming Collegiate Institute, which is to the right of the church. The land was donated by W.E. Jackson, and he, along with his son-in-law, Lemuel Martin, fired the bricks on the Jackson homestead for both the church and school building. (BHCHS-BTM.)

BIG HORN CITY, JOHNSON COUNTY, WYOMING TERRITORY, 1884. The James Gang dugout is located in the creek bank, near the center. Prior to and during the settling of the town, the infamous James Gang frequented old hideouts. A second one is out of view but was located north of the fence, according to Leroy Sackett, an early pioneer and landowner. The James Gang most likely had several different locations for camps, taking advantage of washouts, caves, and other such dwellings. (BHCHS-BTM.)

BIG HORN CITY IN THE WINTER OF 1883–1884. This photograph was taken during the winter from Sackett's Hill east of Big Horn City on the Bozeman Trail. The wagon trail winds down the hill, then turns left to cross Little Goose Creek below the blacksmith shop. Note that the mountain slopes are barren of trees. A buffalo skull sits in the middle of the road between the wagon tracks. (BHCHS-BTM.)

BIG HORN CITY, WYOMING, 1893.
The Wyoming Collegiate Institute,
located on the hill in the center of
this photograph, was the idea of "a
group of citizens who not only sought
greater educational advantages,
but who felt it would enhance
property values in the community
as well. The community was to sell
scholarships to support the institution
financially, and the Congregational
Missionary Society would provide the
instructors and program," as noted
in Deck Hunter's Big Horn City
books, volume 2. (BHCHS-BTM.)

THE REVEREND JENNINGS. The
Jennings family arrived in Big Horn
City in the spring of 1885. Victoria
Jennings passed away in 1889, leaving
the reverend with four small children.
He soon remarried and homesteaded
on Kruse Creek. By 1902, his marriage
dissolved, he sold his property to George
Skinner, and he was sent to serve the
Congregational church in Nampa,
Idaho. (Chuck Custis and John Custis.)

BERT ECKERSON AND PALS. A young Bert Eckerson is seated in front with his friends with Grover Hough standing at the left and Bones Taylor on the right. Bert was the eldest son of William and Florence Eckerson. He was born on August 28, 1895. He married Leona Berniece Evans. Bert passed away on August 10, 1971, and is buried in the Sheridan Municipal Cemetery. (Donna Eckerson Angel.)

HOOF BRANDING. On the back of this old photograph from around 1920 is written, "Bill Eckerson (hoof branding), Don Eckerson (corral hand), British Cavalry Inspection World War I." Bill had worked as a stagecoach driver between Buffalo and Ohlman, Wyoming, in the 1880s. At one time, he was a foreman for Oliver H. Wallop. (Donna Eckerson Angel.)

FLORENCE BELLE DARLING
ECKERSON. In 1887, the Darling
family traveled west by wagon train
from Lundy's Lane, Pennsylvania,
which was also the birthplace
of Florence. Florence married
W.H. Eckerson in 1895, and
the couple settled in Big Horn
City, buying the Thomas Green
home, which is still owned by
the Eckerson family. Florence is
standing behind her father, David,
and her mother, Thirza Darling.
(Donna Eckerson Angel.)

JULY 31, 1891. This rare
photograph was labeled as Big
Horn, Wyoming–July 31, 1891.
The stagecoach is decorated and
has a few passengers. The road
used to go northeast from the
Big Horn Mercantile towards the
S-curve around the riverbed of
Little Goose Creek. No one is
identified in the photograph. The
stagecoach was most probably
one that belonged to the Rock
Creek Stage Line. (WYRM.)

JEROME AND CLEMENTINE BROWN.
Jerome F. Brown, known as "Cheese Brown," married Clementine Almeda Martin in Danville, Illinois, around 1863. They moved to Big Horn City on October 10, 1887. He was a postmaster, rancher, and county commissioner in Johnson County. He was serving as a commissioner during the Johnson County Cattle War. They later moved back to the Big Horn area. (Brown Collection, BHCHS-BTM.)

BUFFALO, WYOMING, DECEMBER 16, 1891. This excerpt from the Johnson County Commissioner's Minutes reads, "County Commissioners met in special session . . . being present D.J. Hogerson and J.F. Brown . . . Upon Motion it is ordered that a reward of $5,000.00 be offered for the arrest and conviction of the murderer or Murderers of O.E. Jones and J.A. Tisdale or $2,500.00 for the arrest and conviction of the murder of either one of them." (Johnson County Commissioner's Minutes.)

O.P. HANNA, 1926. Oliver Perry Hanna sits in Vie Willits Garber's buggy. The Hanna family left Wyoming in 1915 and moved to Long Beach, California. Oliver returned for a visit in 1926 to attend the 50th anniversary of Custer's Last Stand. This photograph was taken in July at J.O. Willits's birthday party, held at the Willitses' stone house. He was the founding father of Big Horn City. (Victor Garber family.)

GUS AND ROSA OLSON FAMILY, C. 1919. August Olson immigrated to America in 1907 from Sweden. He made his way to northern Wyoming, working in railroad tie camps. He married Rosa Hepp on April 26, 1913. This photograph was taken shortly after they moved to Big Horn. Pictured, from left to right, are their children, Inga, born in 1917; Bessie, born in 1914; and Harry, born in 1918. Another son died at birth in 1916. (Gary McCoy.)

HENRY AND SARAH TOWNSEND
FAMILY. Henry and Sarah Baxter
Townsend moved to Wyoming
shortly after this photograph was
taken in 1886. They arrived in
Big Horn City on July 4, 1888, via
a prairie schooner drawn by four
mules. It took them one month
to make the trip from Kansas
as they drove their cattle along
with them. The three children
in back are Dora Ann (left),
William David, and Rosa Maola
(right). Mabel Lucretia is sitting on
Sarah's lap with Edward Sherman
sitting on the bench. Edward
remembers walking behind the
wagon on the trek from Kansas.
The portrait below was taken most
likely in the early 1900s to mark
their 30th wedding anniversary.
Another photograph exists of
the couple in their later years.
(Both, James H. Townsend.)

Kusel Cousins Marry Townsend Sisters.
Cousins Fred and John Kusel married sisters
Ella and Ruby Townsend. The double
wedding took place on December
23, 1905. John and Ruby are on
the right. Ella and Ruby were
daughters of Henry and Sarah
Townsend. Ruby was only 15
when she was married. (James
H. Townsend.)

Beckton Flour Mill.
Edward and Benitta
Townsend purchased the
Beckton Flour Mill and
operated it until 1923. The
mill was powered by water
from Big Goose Creek and
ground flour from Wyoming
wheat. The Townsend children
are in the photograph playing in
the water. Edward helped organize
the Northern Wyoming Poultry
Association and was the first in this
section to breed and exhibit poultry.
(James H. Townsend.)

EDWARD AND BENITTA TOWNSEND, C. 1920. Edward Townsend and Benitta Helen Dow eloped, traveling by train to be married in the Methodist parsonage at Billings on January 10, 1906. Benitta, born September 6, 1889, was adopted by Jack and Helen Dow. Edward was born on September 20, 1882. Benitta and Edward raised six children: Berniece, born in 1908; Edward, born in 1911; Peggy, born in 1913; James, born in 1924; Dora, born in 1928; and Roy, born in 1932. (James H. Townsend.)

OLIVER HENRY AND MARGUERITE WALLOP. Oliver H. Wallop came to the Little Goose Valley in 1891 and purchased O.P. Hanna's homestead. He later purchased the William "Bear" Davis ranch and named it the Canyon Ranch, which is still owned and operated by the Wallop family. Oliver H. Wallop was a cousin to Malcolm and William Moncreiffe, who were from Scotland and later settled on ranches near the Wallop land. (BHCHS-BTM.)

JIM KEMP. James H. Kemp homesteaded south of Big Horn on Kemp Creek. Kemp Flats and Kemp Creek were named for this man. He was born in England and had one brother, Frank. On the back of this photograph, taken June 12, 1904, are the names of the horses: Don Whiskeroso, the pack horse, and Toby, the saddle horse. The notation on the back also states the photograph was taken by E.J. Cameron, Terry, Montana. (Donna Eckerson Angel.)

EMMA AND WILLIAM SACKETT. This is the wedding photograph of Emma Watkins and William Wallace Sackett, taken on March 30, 1898. They had six children. Their homestead was south of Big Horn on Trabing Creek. They later owned the Makinley Wood farm and later still the Hurlbutt ranch, which is more commonly known as Hidden Valley Ranch. (Sackett Collection, BHCHS-BTM.)

HUGH AND LEE SACKETT. This Sackett homestead near Mayoworth in Johnson County was operated by Hugh (man at left). His family is at far left: (from left to right) Ethel, Brennis, Vance, and Lee. The man standing by the wagon is unidentified. Hugh was the sixth child of John and Martha Sackett, who had homesteaded near Big Horn City in 1880. (Marcia Haworth Collection.)

LEROY SACKETT. This photograph of Leroy was taken at the foot of the schoolhouse hill, looking southwest towards the Wyoming Collegiate Institute. He is a young boy dressed in a derby hat with a large ruffled bow on his shirt. His pants appear to be knickers. The picture was taken in 1903 using a camera with glass negatives. (Sackett Collection, BHCHS-BTM.)

THE W.W. SACKETT FAMILY. William Wallace Sackett and his wife, Emma, are pictured with their children around 1909. Standing from left to right are Leroy, Sula, Mabel, and Dorothy. The couple lost one son, Harold, in 1902. Another daughter was born later. William died on November 25, 1915, leaving his young family for Emma to raise. (Sackett Collection, BHCHS-BTM.)

"SOLDIERS GOING PAST OUR HOUSE." When the Sacketts lived south of Big Horn, this photograph was taken of a detail of soldiers hauling what appears to be wood or hay. The old Bozeman Trail passed just south of Big Horn City through the Sackett ranch. This photograph has been reprinted from a glass negative. (Sackett Collection, BHCHS-BTM.)

FAMOUS ARTIST M.D. HOUGHTON'S PANORAMIC SKETCH, 1905. Merritt Dana Houghton sketched several early Wyoming towns. The location of the original sketch is unknown, but luckily Jack Pelissier and Dave Parker have given copies to the Bozeman Trail Museum. (BHCHS-BTM.)

"SCHOOL TEACHER WITH 6 SHOOTER." The schoolteacher is not identified, but the woman standing in the middle is Mattie Blaney, with her husband, Oliver, more commonly known as "Dan," at right. The little girl is Edith. Oliver and Mattie had seven children. She worked at the Gallatin ranch as a maidservant, cook, and seamstress. (Maurine Badgett.)

FULLER STUDIO. These three young men were the graduating class of 1919 at the Big Horn School. Standing in back is Glenn Parker. Seated at left is Richard Marquess, with Norman Custis on the right. Their motto was, "Not how much, but how well." The photograph was taken in Sheridan at the Fuller Studio. (Donna Eckerson Angel.)

FANCY LADIES. These ladies are all dressed up in their best clothes, including fancy hats. It must have been a special occasion to have these five ladies meet in a studio for this photograph, taken around 1911. From left to right are Minerva Bard, Minnie Martin, Alice Skinner, and Mrs. George Webster. Ella Jackson is in front with what appears to be her left hand moving up to her face. (BHCHS-BTM.)

GATCHELL PHARMACY CELEBRATION. The 50th anniversary of the Gatchell Drug Store brought together the Gatchell family for this rare photograph. The date was May 22, 1950. Standing in front are Jim and Ursula (Sackett) Gatchell. Their daughters are standing in back, from left to right: Clare, Genevieve, and Thelma. (Marcia Haworth Collection.)

THE EMIL BENSON FAMILY. Emil Benson and Lora Hepp were married on April 30, 1917. Oscar was born on July 13, 1918, and Sheila was born on September 26, 1920. Later, two more daughters joined the family, Phyllis in 1930 and Karleen in 1936. A set of twins died at birth in 1926. Emil and Lora always had room to feed extra folks at the dinner table. (Gary McCoy.)

WYOMING COLLEGIATE INSTITUTE, 1892. William E. Jackson, who donated the land and bricks for the Wyoming Collegiate Institute, stands in the doorway. "Professor H. N. Robinson is standing near corner," as described in the 1959 *Big Horn Pioneers* book. The bell is now property of the Bozeman Trail Museum. (BHCHS-BTM.)

GRADUATING CLASS OF THE WYOMING COLLEGIATE INSTITUTE, 1897. The first (and only) class to graduate from the Wyoming Collegiate Institute is, from left to right, Sula J. Sackett, Carl L. Sackett, Edna M. Jackson, and J.M. White seated. Sula became the wife of James Gatchell of Buffalo. Carl became a US district attorney. Edna became a doctor. J.M. White served as a US law clerk in Washington, DC. (BHCHS-BTM.)

THINGS REQUIRED

1. Prompt attention is required at all enjoined exercises of the Institute and at all recitations.
2. A respectful and courteous demeanor towards all instuctors.
3. A due respect and courtesy toward all associates, citizens, and strangers.
4. A proper observance of the Sabbath, regular attendance at church and Sunday School, morning and evening, at such place of worship as the parents shall designate.
5. All students are required to be in their rooms at study from 7 till 9 o'clock p. m. and to retire not later than 9:30 p. m.

THINGS PROHIBITED

6. All profane and obscene language.
7. Loafing about places of amusement.
8. Riding, walking, or engaging in any kind of amusement during study hours.
9. Injury to Institute property.
10. Use of tobacco about Institute building or grounds, and all use of intoxicating drinks, and carrying arms.
11. Leaving town without permission.
12. Playing at games of chance.
13. Riding out with the opposite sex, and attending parties of pleasure without permission.
14. Visiting or receiving visits from the opposite sex, or keeping company with those not connected with the Institute, without permission.
15. Receiving or giving instructions in any branch taught in the Institute from others than members of the faculty without consent.

Further information will be gladly given by addressing,

CHARLES ANDERSON, Principal,
Big Horn, Wyoming.

THINGS REQUIRED, THINGS PROHIBITED. The list of things required of the students who attended the Wyoming Collegiate Institute included "due respect and courtesy toward all associates, citizens, and strangers" and "all students are required to be in their rooms at study from 7 till 9 o'clock p.m. and to retire not later than 9:30 p.m." (BHCHS-BTM.)

CHRISTMAS DAY, 1925. Leroy Sackett and Bessie Collins were married on December 25, 1925. They celebrated their 50th wedding anniversary in 1975 at the Big Horn Woman's Club. Bessie wore this original wedding gown at the 50th anniversary celebration. (BHCHS-BTM.)

BERTHA AND CLYDE SACKETT. Clyde Sackett was the son of John and Martha. He was born on August 20, 1880, in Cheyenne. This would have been just two months prior to John coming to Big Horn City to establish the Sackett and Skinner Mercantile business. Bertha Fleming was born in 1887. Clyde was a polo player for the early Moncreiffe teams and worked as a cowboy. (BHCHS-BTM.)

MRS. FRANK KEMP AND FRANK II. This photograph was taken on November 9, 1893, at the Rinehart Studios. On the back is written "With love from—Little Frank—taken on his third birthday." Frank was Jim Kemp's brother. The picture was found in the Eckerson Photograph Collection. (Donna Eckerson Angel.)

THE KUSEL FAMILY. Johann Heinrich Wilhelm Kusel (William Sr., at right) and his wife, Dorothea Louise Sophie Ihde (at left), are pictured with their three oldest children in this faded photograph taken at the L.B. Glafcke Studio in Sheridan, Wyoming. Standing from left to right are Friedrich Heinrich Wilhelm, George Christian Ludwig, and their sister, Louisa Maria Sophia. William purchased the Leo Lambrigger homestead. (BHCHS-BTM)

MALCOLM MONCREIFFE. He was the 15th of 16 children, born in Scotland to Sir Thomas and Lady Louisa Moncreiffe. Malcolm settled in the Little Goose Valley in 1898 and became involved in the sheep and horse ranching business. He furnished the British cavalry horses for the Boer War in South Africa. (BHCHS-BTM.)

BRADFORD BRINTON AND HIS STAGECOACH, C. 1928. Jessamine Spear Johnson was the photographer who took this black-and-white print. Her signature brand is in the lower right corner. Two men and two women are in the horse-drawn stagecoach parked in a field on the Bradford Brinton ranch, more commonly known as the Quarter Circle A. (WYRM.)

WILLIAM MONCREIFFE. William, the older brother of Malcolm Moncreiffe, came to the United States and became a naturalized citizen. His homestead patent was received on December 7, 1912. He built the stately white house that later became known as the Bradford Brinton Memorial. He sold part of his ranch to Goelet Gallatin of New York and the remaining portion to Bradford Brinton in 1925. (WYRM.)

81

COWBOYS, C. 1894. These 11 cowboys are identified as follows on the back of the picture: "left to right: H.W. (Doc) Spear, Bill Glasgow (brother of Jim, moved to Cody), Andy Martin (Sheridan), Lew Burgess (Judge Burgess's uncle), Nelson Darlington (Big Horn pioneer), Guy Wood (Elsa's cousin, Mrs. Willits' son-in-law, Guy lived with Mrs. Willits after wife died, Iris Hick's father), unknown, William (Bill) Eckerson (Big Horn pioneer), Aaron Darlington (Big Horn pioneer),

BLACKSMITH SHOP. This was the building that housed the Big Horn Sentinel newspaper print shop, built in 1884. The building was owned by Charles and Minerva Bard in 1887, shortly after the newspaper moved to Buffalo. Later the building became a blacksmith shop after it was purchased by Lance "Brownie" Sinsel in 1937. It is currently owned by John Drake, who has remodeled the building to resemble its pioneer days. (BHCHS-BTM.)

unknown, unknown." These cowboys were most likely working for the Moncreiffe and Wallop partnership in gathering and training horses for the British cavalry. More than 25,000 horses were brought to the Little Goose Valley for inspection before being sent to South Africa. The entire community benefited from the horse ranching for several years until the automobile came along. (WYRM.)

BIG GOOSE STAGE CROSSING, 1896. The crossing was a busy stopping place, since it was most likely the only saloon on the mountain road from Big Horn City to Hyattville. It was also referred to as the "Morrow Stage Station." The stage station was operated by Fertig and Benefield on Mondays, Wednesdays, and Fridays. The cost for a single fare was $5.50 for the 27-hour-long trip. (WYRM.)

TREELESSNESS, "THE TOWN OF BIG HORN, WYOMING, JULY 30, 1901." The Oriental Hotel is at left; across the street are the Star of the West Saloon, the Big Horn Mercantile Warehouse and Mercantile, the Last Chance Saloon (now known as the Bozeman Trail Inn), Big Horn Saloon, and the Hathaway Building. (W.O. Clough Collection, negative No. 1845, photo files, Wyoming–Big Horn, American Heritage Center, University of Wyoming.)

BIG HORN, 1926. Elsa Spear Byron took many photographs of Big Horn over the years. This one is labeled "Big Horn, Wyoming, lined with false front buildings." Six of the buildings remain standing today: the Order of Odd Fellows hall; the Dewitt blacksmith shop, which serves as a museum; the Moreland house; the Big Horn Mercantile Warehouse and Mercantile; and the Bozeman Trail Inn. (Elsa Spear Byron Collection at WYRM.)

Two

LIVELIHOOD

THE ICE CUTTERS. This is from a glass slide negative taken by Virginia Belle Benton Spear. It was taken on one of the ponds on the Spear Ranch. The blocks of ice were packed in piles of straw and stored to be used in the summertime. Many small icehouses were built in the town for community use. It was truly a community work project. (Elsa Spear Byron Collection at WYRM.)

PICNIC IN THE MOUNTAINS. W.E. Jackson is the gentleman sitting near the tent in the background. He served as the first Bighorn Forest Reserve supervisor. The little boy at left holds a fishing pole, while the woman on the right holds a rifle. (WYRM.)

ELDERLY WOMAN FISHING. This pole must be 12 feet long. Fishing was a way for everyone to add meat to the dinner table. The unidentified lady wears her Sunday bonnet and long dress. This photograph was first printed in the May 1916 issue of *The Teepee Book: Sportman's Number*, published by Herbert Coffeen. (CHIEF, INC.)

CHARLIE DAVIS OF PASS CREEK. A nephew of the Davises from Big Horn, Charlie Davis was a great hunter "and never fails to get his bear every fall or winter," as noted on the back of the photograph. The women are wearing their Sunday best dresses and bonnets. Charlie is also wearing a dress shirt. His chaps are fancy with long curly hair, most likely bear hide, which makes his legs look thick. (CHIEF, INC.)

ERNEST HEMINGWAY AT FOLLEY RANCH. Searching for a quiet place to finish his book A *Farewell to Arms*, Ernest Hemingway came west in the summer of 1928. He stayed at the Sheridan Inn, Folley Ranch, and ended up at the Spear-O-Wigwam. He is seen here with another guest seated on the running board of his yellow Ford Roadster. In August, his second wife, Pauline, and six-week-old son Patrick joined him. (WYRM)

STRING OF PACK HORSES. This string of pack horses is led by Jessamine Spear Johnson. This was the mode of transportation for visiting the high country in the Bighorn Mountains. Jessamine managed the Spear-O-Wigwam dude ranch from 1930 until 1943. (*String of Pack Horses*, by Jessamine Spear Johnson. May not be used without the permission of X4, LLC. This photograph may be protected by copyright law.)

SKIING. These folks had tree limb ski poles and wide wooden skis. One lady has snowshoes, and, of course, the females are wearing dresses. The skis are strapped on with leather bindings around their boots. These were most likely the early version of the cross-country telemark skis of today. (CHIEF, INC.)

POLO IN THE COWBOY STATE. Frank Wood was a cowboy, and on some occasions, he played polo. This photograph shows the equipment of an early-20th-century polo player. The sport has been played in the Little Goose Valley since the early 1900s. (Marce Lee Nelson.)

KNITTING AND READING. Grace Snow is sitting on a rock knitting while her friend Ruth Spear reads a book. They were in the mountains on a camping trip. This may have been a familiar pastime in the early 1900s, since so many young ladies were encouraged to engage in needlework and also to read. Books were scarce, so it was common to share books among families. (CHIEF, INC.)

DIRT WORK ON PARK RESERVOIR.
Park Reservoir was first built in
1910. This scraper was used in
September 1932 when repairing
Park Reservoir. As witnessed
by Victor Garber when he was
a young boy, "Teams of horses
pulling from the front and pushing
from the back would be moving
constantly as the wagons carrying
off the excess dirt came next to
the scraper at a full run." (Bowman
Collection, BHCHS-BTM.)

STOUT'S SHEEP. These are sheep
belonging to the Stout family
coming down Red Grade Road
after being in the mountains
while grazing during the summer
months. (*Stout's Sheep*, by
Jessamine Spear Johnson. May not
be used without the permission
of X4, LLC. This photograph may
be protected by copyright law.)

BIG HORN MOUNTAIN SPORTS: FISHING AND HORSEBACK RIDING. Torrey Johnson fishes from his horse Reno. Torrey is a descendant of two Big Horn pioneer families. He is the great-grandson of Rev. George Washington and Hannah Benton and Willys and Jane Spear and the son of Jessamine Spear Johnson. (*Torrey Fishing*, by Jessamine Spear Johnson. May not be used without the permission of X4, LLC. This photograph may be protected by copyright law.)

EVEN LITTLE GIRLS GET TO GO ON PACK TRIPS. In 1911, Willis Moses Spear took 34 people on a two-week-long pack trip. Annabelle and Phyllis Johnson, daughters of Will and Jessamine Johnson, were two of the youngest in the group. They were tied to their saddles with rope so they could take naps while riding the trail. (*Pack Trip*, by Jessamine Spear Johnson. Used by permission of the Johnson family and X4, LLC. © 2011, X4, LLC, all rights reserved.)

ANOTHER ONE BITES THE DUST ON RED GRADE ROAD. While driving up Red Grade Road, suitcases bounced out of the back of this truck. The driver fixes the board tailgate while the family car waits before heading up the grade to Spear-O-Wigwam on top of the mountain near Cross Creek. (*Red Grade Road*, by Jessamine Spear Johnson. Used by permission of the Johnson family and X4, LLC. © 2011, X4, LLC, all rights reserved.)

BENTON CAVE IN LITTLE GOOSE CANYON. Torrey Johnson, right, and an unidentified guest take a rest. To access the cave, one must hike and climb quite a distance. These folks most likely rode horses several miles from the Spear-O-Wigwam. The Spear family built the guest ranch in 1922 and operated it until April 1943. (*Benton Cave*, by Jessamine Spear Johnson. May not be used without the permission of X4, LLC. This photograph may be protected by copyright law.)

Three

GROUP ACTIVITIES

NOVEMBER 3, 1940, CLOUD PEAK REBEKAH LODGE NO. 14'S "GOLDEN JUBILEE." Pictured are, from left to right, (first row) Kathleen Langelier, Rae Mela, Florence Affeldt, Grace Bentley, Vera Francis, Vie Garber, Dorothy Skinner, Mrs. Waltman, and Anna Nottingham; (second row) Modine Skinner, Mrs. Ralph Crandall, Jennie Parker, Mae Furber, Emma Dow, Hazel McGovern, Marguerite Garber, Mrs. Lucas, Mary Perry, Bessie Sackett, Lora Benson (?), Alice Hansen, Meta Connell, Edith Gallatin, and Opal Lovelace. (BHCHS-BTM.)

CLOUD PEAK PACK TRIP, JULY 10, 1911. There were 34 people and 57 horses on this pack trip. Those on the trip included nine members of the Willis M. Spear family, four members of the John B. Kendrick family, four members of the John Eddy family, Harry Kay, Ralph Thomas, Porter Doak, Phillip Miles, Frank Rarick, Mr. Mintz, Charles Helvey, Howard King, Nell Skinner, Ona Toland, Doris Munford, Hazel Helvey, Stella Benton, Ruby Stevenson, Cordelia Leamon, Peyton Kincel, and Bill Gollings. (Elsa Spear Byron Collection at WYRM.)

SHERIDAN CORNET BAND. Three members of this band were early Big Horn City residents: Herbert Coffeen, Tom Tynan, and Henry Gerdel. Band members are, from left to right, (first row) J. Frank Heald, Herbert Coffeen, Tom Tynan, Harry Neely, and Charles Thurmond; (second row) two unidentified men, Mike Burns, M. Matthews, Henry Gerdel, Art Clubb, Bill Barron, Fay Pettit, Oscar Collier, Dick Weaver, and band president Colonel Ferguson. (SCM.)

94

4-H Club. These 4-H club members are proud to display the American flag and their 4-H club emblem. The photograph states "July 1956." Pictured, from left to right, are Frances Genereaux, Shirley Garland, Janet Garland, Mary Kay Slack, Leader Jackie Slack, Tom Logan, Judy Mills, Roberta Moore, and Judy Barrett. (Frances Hansen.)

Old Timers Picnic, June 1959. Some of Big Horn's early settlers gathered for a picnic at Fred Hilman's ranch. Pictured, from left to right, are Nancy Burns Brooks, Bertha Fleming Sackett, Don Eckerson, Madge Austin Wade, Bert Eckerson, Maud Skinner Langheldt, Edith Gerdel Knodl, Belle Gerdel Goodrich, Vie Willits Garber, Jessamine Spear Johnson, and Edna Kilbourne Stewart. This photograph was taken by Archie Nash. (BHCHS-BTM.)

JULY 21, 1926. From left to right are Mrs. Harbison, Martha Benton, Helen Dow, Lydia Hilman Davis, Maude Skinner, unidentified, May Davis Howard, J.O. Willits (wearing hat), Miss Howard, Vie Willits Garber, Mrs. Will Davis, Mrs. Shell, Bert Dow (tallest man in back), two unidentified,

JULY 21, 1926. From left to right are, with the date they arrived in Big Horn in parentheses, (first row) Jenny Hilman Davis (1879), Amanda Davis Jackson (1880), Jo Skinner (1885), and "Auntie" Helen Dow (1880); (second row) Lydia Davis Hilman (1879), Mae Davis Howard (1879), Minnie Martin (1880), James Orr Willits (1881), John Custis (1882), Oliver Perry Hanna (1878), Mr. Austin (1881), Joseph Darlington (1882), and Aaron Darlington (1882). (Victor Garber family.)

Jo Skinner, Amanda Davis Jackson, Minnie Jackson Martin (in the black hat), two unidentified, O.P. Hanna, John Custis, Mrs. Austin, Roy Benton, Miss Austin, Aaron Darlington, Jenny Hilman Davis, Mrs. Fitzgerald, and Mr. Austin. (BHCHS-BTM.)

A GATHERING AT THE WOMAN'S CLUB. This group photograph of a gathering of Big Horn folks was taken in the early 1950s, possibly by local photographer Alois Schmidt. From left to right are (first row) Ruby Townsend Kusel, Bertha Fleming Sackett, Irene Shreve, two unidentified, Harry Smith, Grace Smith, and Lora Hepp Benson; (second row) Alice Daly, Loretta Genereaux, Anna Schmidt, Nell Davis, Alice Holstedt, two unidentified, and Louise DeJarnett; (third row) George Ostrom, Pat Powers, Gladys Ostrom, Richard Davis, Carlene Benson, Clara White, unidentified, Joe Genereaux (in back), Helen Currie, unidentified, Walter Bales, Jack Currie, Helen Edmiston, Elzie Edmiston, Patty Edmiston, unidentified, Mrs. and Mr. Walt Bales, and Margaret Powers. (BHCHS-BTM.)

CROGHAN AND TOWNSEND FAMILY REUNION. Seated in the front are Henry and Sarah Townsend. Second from right in the back row is "Auntie" Helen Dow, and standing to her right is her adopted son, Bert Dow. Jack and Helen Dow had also adopted Benitta in the late 1800s, who was, at the time this photograph was taken, married to Ed Townsend, standing in the back row near the center. (BHCHS-BTM.)

DEDICATION OF THE SUNDIAL MARKING BIG HORN CITY'S FIRST CABIN. The Big Horn Woman's Club dedicated this sundial to commemorate the location of Oliver Perry Hanna's cabin site. Pictured are, from left to right, Beth Dunlap, Minnie Martin, Dora Hanna, unidentified, Lydia Hilman, Mrs. Van Dyke, Jo Skinner, Mrs. L.H. Brooks, Mrs. Barton Barnes, Mrs. Davis, and Vie Garber. The dedication was possibly in 1928, fifty years after Hanna built his cabin. (BHCHS-BTM.)

AT THE BAR V RANCH, 1936. From left to right, Emma Dewitt, Lydia Hilman, and Dora Hanna stand in front of a white frame house at the Bar V Ranch. Lydia (pronounced *Lida*) Hilman was the daughter of William "Bear" Davis. He married Jenny Hilman after his first wife died. Therefore, Lydia's stepmother was also her sister-in-law. Lydia can always be identified by the high-collared dresses she wore. (WYRM.)

ANOTHER GATHERING AT THE WOMAN'S CLUB. Pictured are, from left to right, (first row) Mrs. Fred Hilman, Mary Helvey, and Gayle Miech; (second row) Fred Bard, Maud Langheldt, Nell Skinner, Mabel Bard, Helen Currie, Melvine Rolston, and Melvine's granddaughter Leslie; (third row) Bob Harper (young boy), Fred Hilman, Mary Harper, Pauline Hanslip, Purve Langelier, Bob Helvey, Kathy Johns, Amy Miller, Vera Coates, Ollie Joseph, Iris Hicks, Vie Garber, and Gouverneur Skinner. (Currie family.)

NORMAN PERRY IN HIS EVERYDAY CLOTHES, 1954. The ladies were dressed up in pioneer clothing for a celebration. However, Norman always wore the same "old fashioned" clothes. Hazel Bundy is on the left, and Dorothy Skinner is on the right. Norman walked to Sheridan about once a week. Big Horn folks would stop and offer him a ride. Whether he accepted or not depended on the weather. (Currie family.)

NEIGHBORLY GATHERING, 1921. Pictured are, from left to right, (first row) J.O. Willits with Orr Gerber on his lap, Mrs. Davis, Helen Dow with Victor Garber seated in front of her, and Hattie Willits; (second row) Guy Wood, Vie Garber, Vera Wood, Beth Wood, Iris Wood, Roy Garber (hat), and Chip Wood; (third row) Bert Dow and Will Davis. (Victor Garber family.)

REBEKAH LODGE. The Big Horn Rebekah Lodge served the community for nearly 75 years. Pictured are, from left to right, Bertha Sackett, Melvine Rolston, Eva Dewey, Rose Griffith, Betty Eckerson, Alma Long, Mary Robinson, Dorothy Mortenson, Opal Long, Doris Arndt, Louise DeJarnett, Ollie Joseph, Ora Norris, Bessie Fronaphel, Margaret Logan, Mae Furber, and Margaret Powers. (BHCHS-BTM.)

WOMAN'S CLUB PIONEER DAY. Another celebration of the pioneer history of Big Horn City was commemorated by the Big Horn Woman's Club. This group of ladies stands south of the old blacksmith shop that now serves as the Bozeman Trail Museum. Pictured are, from left to right, Mrs. Olin Rose, unidentified, Bette Berry, Gretchen Nelson, Bessie Sackett, Patty Warner, Lora Benson, Louise DeJarnett, Benitta Townsend, Dee Sackett, and Perve Langelier. (BHCHS-BTM.)

CLYDE ROLSTON FAMILY, C. 1920. Pictured are, from left to right, (first row) De Arv, Les, Dorothy, Clifton, and Don; (second row) Elsie, Clyde, Mamie, and Maurice. Les was married to Melvine Bobbitt on September 24, 1935. Don and his family also lived in the Big Horn area. In 1942, Don packed up all their belongings and moved to Washington State. (Bob Rolston.)

SKINNER FAMILY PICNIC IN THE BIGHORN MOUNTAINS, 1893. Pictured are, from left to right, Nellie, Alice, Jo, Rae, Maud, Nell, Bell, Fred, and Charley; (second row) George, Al, John, Bob sitting on Will's lap, and Ben. There is a small track at the base of the hill that might have been

LENSMEN CAMERA CLUB, 1946. Don Diers is the tall man in the back row wearing a coat and tie. Elsa Spear Byron is to his right. Archie Nash is standing fourth from the left, and Mrs. Nash, in a black suit, is sitting at right on the arm of the couch. Alois Schmidt is standing second from left. Elsa, Archie, and Alois were professional photographers from Big Horn. (WYRM.)

used to assist in hauling wood to their lumberyard. (George Harper and family in honor of Charles Skinner's granddaughter Mary.)

FIRE DEPARTMENT ANNUAL DINNER, 1957. Pictured are, from left to right, Victor Slack, Nick Moore, Wendell Loomis, Mrs. Oliver Wallop (facing toward the window), Mr. and Mrs. Dag Haugen, Bill Scobee, Elzie Edmiston, Glen Blackburn, Mr. and Mrs. Jim Berry (near the wall), Mr. and Mrs. Daryl Daly, Mr. and Mrs. Andy Kukuchka, Bernice Norskog, Mr. and Mrs. Harry Adsit with baby Sharon, and Mr. and Mrs. Keith Salisberry. (Big Horn Fire Department.)

FIRE DEPARTMENT ANNUAL DINNER. In 1959, the Big Horn Volunteer Fire Department held its annual dinner in the basement of the youth center, which is the old brick Congregational church. Pictured are, from left to right, Wyla Loomis, Gary Garrett, Warren Bard, Jim Berry, and Andy Kukuchka. Notice the men are wearing the aprons. At least Coors beer and Folgers coffee were on the menu, as seen in this photograph. (Big Horn Fire Department.)

FIRE TRUCK INSPECTION, 1959. Pictured are, from left to right, Elzie Edmiston, Joe Genereaux, Victor Slack, Fred Bard, and Gil Valdez. Earlier in the 1950s, the metal hut was built to house the fire equipment. Possibly one of the first fires to be fought using this truck was the Teepee Lodge fire. It was in the early 1950s and occurred at night. (Big Horn Fire Department.)

THE BIG HORN WOMAN'S CLUB, 2005. The program was called "Easter Parade of Hats," and the ladies wore hats from Bette Berry's collection. Pictured are, from left to right, (first row) Rene Adams, Wyla Loomis, Gwen Turner, Cathy Wallick, Melvine Rolston, and Bette Berry; (second row) Barbara Niner, Wyla Loomis's sister, Elaine Hilman, Karol Meineke, Loraine Lowe, Ann Custis, Joyce Clemons, Helen Currie, Janet Shepherd, Janet Berry, and Karen Stears. (John Berry.)

BIG HORN FIRE DEPARTMENT. Once again the Big Horn Fire Department gather for a photograph with their new truck. Pictured are, from left to right, Clayton Dewey, Kenneth Sackett, Leroy Sackett, Richard Marquess, Foster Bundy, Joe Genereaux, Fred Bard, Lee Garrett, Jack Broderick, Ronald Wyatt, and Alois Schmid. Kneeling in front are Les Rolston (left) and Merle Blair. (Big Horn Fire Department.)

BIG HORN HIGH SCHOOL, 1951. The 1951 Big Horn High School graduates combined with the 4-H club to pose for this photograph. Pictured are, from left to right (first row) Vie Garber, Pat Gleason, Martha Perry, Delores DeJarnett, Alice Davis, and Kathleen O'Conner; (second row) Donna Vandenberg, Sally Talcott (?), Mrs. Tom White, Pat Kay, Melvine Rolston, Donna Bales, Janice White, Jeanne Moreland, Dorothy Kay, and Jo Elaine Holloway. (Melvine Rolston.)

FLOYD COATES'S FAMILY GATHERING. Floyd and Vera Coates dressed up for a special occasion with their young family. This photograph was taken on their place south of Big Horn in approximately 1950. From left to right, Betty, Lily, and George are standing in front, and Mona and Les are in the back. Another daughter, Leta, was born in 1951. (Mona Coates Brown.)

BOY SCOUTS. This photograph was taken by Alois Schmidt of Boy Scout Troop No. 118. Pictured are, from left to right, (first row) David Berry, Leo Baker, Greg Eckerson, and John Arnoux; (second row) Dick Bard, John Currie, Marion Loomis, Kenny Warner, and Virgil Garland; (third row) Scout Master Jack Currie, Jim Currie, Tom Logan, Jim Arnoux, Ben Anderson, Joe Baker, Pete Fry, and Assistant Leader Henry Arnoux. (Currie family.)

PARENTS AT CUB SCOUT HALLOWEEN PARTY, 1958. Pictured are, from left to right, (first row) Mrs. Johnson, Bette Berry, and Jo Moore; (second row) Donna Johnson, Judy Moore, Betty Eckerson, Jackie Slack, Helen Bard, Helen Currie, and Frances Berry; (third row) Patty Warner, Bud Warner, Everett Berry, Victor Slack, Warren Bard, Marion Brayton, Jim Berry, and Mrs. Henry (?). (Currie family.)

CUB SCOUT HALLOWEEN PARTY, 1958. From left to right are (first row) Rick Clabaugh, Mike Brayton, David Moore, Don Norskog, Greg Eckerson, Randy Bannas, John Berry, Bruce Clabaugh (behind John Berry), and Charles Bannas; (second row) Cindy Warner, Judy Currie, Mary Ella Bard, Jody Brayton, Dan Berry, Margie Brayton, Terry Bannas, and Virgil Garland; (third row) Bonnie Warner, Joe Baker, John Currie, Bill Johnson, John Slack, Ken Warner, Dick Bard, Leo Baker, Eddie Moore, Thad Brayton, and Marion Loomis; (fourth row) Mike Berry, Dennis Loomis, Donna Eckerson, Pete Henry, Roberta Moore, and Jim Currie. (Currie family.)

Four

HISTORIANS AND PRESERVATIONISTS

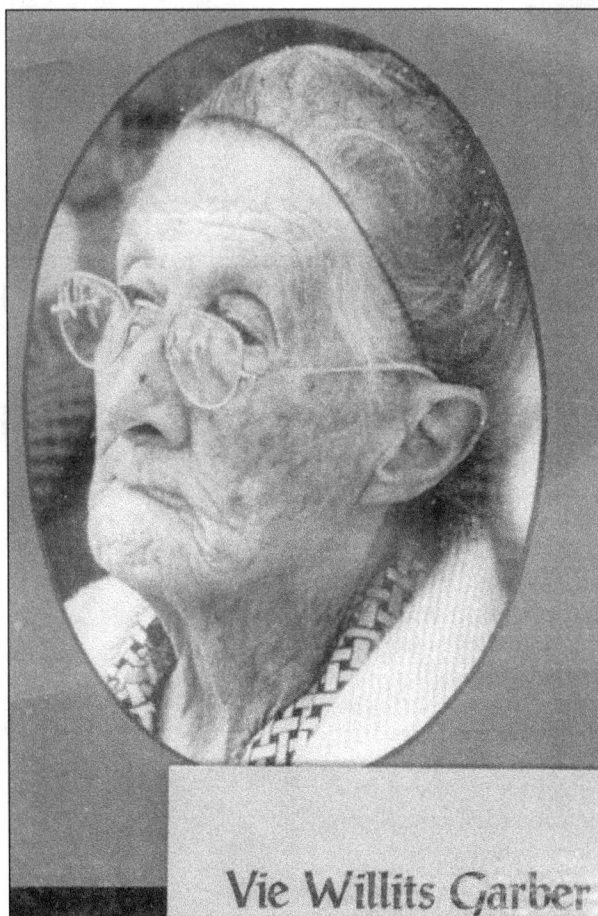

VIE WILLITS GARBER (1884–1985). Big Horn City was the beloved home of Vie Willits Garber for more than 100 years. Born on her parents' homestead, which was called Farview, she was a leading authority on local history and was instrumental in publishing the book *Big Horn Pioneers*, which was written by her high school English classes in 1957–1958. Garber's family continues to carry on the preservation of Big Horn City history. (Victor Garber family.)

Vie Willits Garber

DECK HUNTER (1928–2010). Her five books are highly sought-after and contain rare information. Hunter left the community with several taped interviews of pioneer family members, old record books, homestead records, maps, diaries, letters, photographs, and obituaries. Many of the photographs used in this book were due to her diligence in collecting and preserving copies of the Big Horn City historic record. She was a member of the Big Horn City Historical Society. (JS.)

SALLY SPRINGER (1935–2004) AND ELSA SPEAR BYRON (1896–1992). Two grand ladies of Big Horn City history were Sally Springer and Elsa Spear Byron. Elsa wrote several articles, books, and diaries. Sally nurtured the Big Horn City Historical Society (BHCHS). She helped to secure artifacts for the Bozeman Trail Museum, edited the newsletter for several years, kept records for the Mount Hope Cemetery, and wrote *Big Horn Tidbits of History*. (BHCHS-BTM.)

THE GARBER FAMILY. Pictured are, from left to right, (first row) Abbey, Kathryn, Phillip and Jennifer; (second row) David and Judy Garber, Paul and Saralee Garber, Roy and Nancy Garber, and Tom and Pat Mahon. Phyllis and Victor are seated. The entire family has been dedicated to community work and preserving the family homestead. Roy and Nancy live in the original Willits home, preserving furniture, paintings, clothing, and photographs. (Victor Garber family.)

FROM LEFT TO RIGHT: HELEN CURRIE (1910–2008), BETTE BERRY (1919–2010), AND MELVINE ROLSTON. They worked tirelessly for the Big Horn Woman's Club, Lions Club dinners, Mount Hope Cemetery board, the Big Horn City Historical Society, 4-H clubs, and Boy Scouts and remained close friends for more than 50 years. Melvine's cookbook, *80 Years in the Kitchen*, is one of the Bozeman Trail Museum's best-selling books. They were founding members of the BHCHS. (Currie family.)

ROBERT LEGOSKI. In 2000, Legoski wrote a book titled *General George Crook's Campaign of 1876*. The book includes several drawings of how the Little Goose Valley looked at that time. He includes newspaper articles that cover June 5 through August 3, 1876. It is a wonderful study of life during that fateful summer, which includes the Rosebud and Little Bighorn battles. He is a member of the BHCHS. (Robert Legoski.)

WILLIS MOSES AND VIRGINIA BELLE BENTON SPEAR. The Spear family preserved local history through diaries, letters, scrapbooks, and photographs. This rare snapshot of Willis and Virginia gives a glance at the many hours spent writing in their precious diaries. Elsa wrote on the back of the photograph, "1912 Papa and Mama. I took this in the dining room at 164 Wyoming Avenue with my box brownie camera." (Elsa Spear Byron Collection at WYRM.)

ELSA SPEAR BYRON AND DAUGHTER MARILYN BILYEU. The community is extremely thankful to Marilyn Bilyeu for giving the Elsa Spear Byron Collection to the Wyoming Room at the Sheridan County Public Library. The diaries are a treasure trove of news articles, never-before-seen snapshots, dried flowers, movie tickets, weather reports, food costs, and the books they were reading. Marilyn is a member of the BHCHS. (Elsa Spear Byron Collection at WYRM.)

KAY WALLICK, D.J. PURCELL, AND JOAN AND BOB WALLICK. Bob and Joan (right) are preservationists of local buildings. They have preserved one of Sheridan's earliest homes by moving it south of Big Horn. It is currently being remodeled by D.J. Purcell and his wife, Kay (left). It is located on the site of the old dance hall that burned on September 7, 1924. They are members of the BHCHS and financially support the society. (Wallick family.)

GEORGE AND MARY HARPER. This photograph was taken in 2006 of George and Mary Harper. They have been guardians of the Big Horn Mercantile since Maud Skinner Langheldt passed away. Mary is Charles W. Skinner's granddaughter and Maud's daughter. George and Mary's son Tom and his wife, Holly, are current owners. They are members of the BHCHS. The Big Horn Merc and warehouse are listed on the National Register of Historic Places. (JS.)

SKINNER AND SACKETT DESCENDANTS, 2010. The great-grandson of Charles Skinner, Tom Harper, and the great-great-grandson of John Sackett, Paul Haworth, met at the Big Horn Mercantile. This meeting was about 130 years after the Skinner and Sackett business adventure began. Pictured are, from left to right, current owners Tom and Holly Harper, Paul and Christina Haworth, and their son Nathaniel. The Haworths opened a new grocery store in Sheridan called Sackett's Market. They are all members of the BHCHS. (JS.)

HERBERT COFFEEN IN HIS STORE, THE SIGN OF THE TEEPEE. His most beloved endeavor was the Sign of the Teepee store, located in Sheridan, that sold Indian artifacts. Many of the items seen in this photograph have found their way into the Peabody Museum of Archaeology at Harvard University. Herbert was the son of Henry Asa Coffeen, one of Big Horn City's earliest pioneers and for whom Coffeen Avenue in Sheridan is named. (CHIEF, INC.)

THE MARC COFFEEN FAMILY. An always-generous Marc Coffeen (1946–2007) shared his family collection with the public. This collection has now been preserved in the Coffeen Historical Information Education Foundation (CHIEF, INC). This photograph was taken a short time before Marc's passing. Pictured are, from left to right, Nathan, Quinn, Marc, Trish, and Christopher Coffeen. They are members of the BHCHS. (CHIEF, INC.)

WARREN DeJARNETT. After serving as Big Horn School District's superintendent for many years, Warren retired in 1971. He and his wife, Louise, were involved with the Big Horn community, working on church projects, the volunteer fire department, and the historical preservation of Big Horn City. Warren was the chairman of the bicentennial celebration. He was instrumental in the publication of the *Big Horn Pioneers*. The DeJarnett family has been members of the BHCHS. (BHCHS-BTM.)

JIM BERRY AND FOSTER BUNDY, 1968. Jim, right, and Foster, sitting, were two of the most reliable, hard-working men in Big Horn. Foster worked to build the volunteer fire department and gave to every event and needy family through his generosity as the store manager of the Big Horn Merc. Jim was instrumental in keeping the records and caring for Mount Hope Cemetery, was a volunteer fireman, cooked hamburgers for the Lions Club Carnival, was a Boy Scout leader, and served as secretary-treasurer for the 1976 bicentennial committee. Jim also served as the postmaster of the Big Horn Post Office. Their descendants are members of the BHCHS. (Dan Berry.)

VIE GARBER AND HELEN BRINTON. Two of Big Horn's major preservationists were Vie Willits Garber, seated at left, and Helen Brinton, seated at right. Others are, from left to right, Chip and Roy Garber, Iris Wood Hicks, and Marguerite Garber. Helen preserved the home of her brother Bradford Brinton. It was opened to the public as a museum of Western art, now known as the Bradford Brinton Memorial. (Victor Garber family.)

FLOYD BARD. Two books were written by Floyd about early Big Horn City history. *Horse Wrangler* and *Dude Wrangler* were stories covering more than 60 years of his cowboy life. The books reveal a view of life that is not from the wealthy horse and cattle ranchers but from the mind of a hard-working cowboy who never forgot a horse (or a horse's name). (BHCHS-BTM.)

MARK BADGETT AND HIS MULE JEZEBEL. Mark hiked and camped along the Bozeman Trail, searching for artifacts and learning about its path across Wyoming. He was the descendant of Oliver Daniel Blaney and Mattie Ellen Dickey, who lived and worked in the Big Horn area. His brother Al and sister Maureen are members of the BHCHS. Maureen has worked in the Bozeman Trail Museum, assisting in educating visitors. (Carolyn Badgett.)

GEORGE OSTROM. George Ostrom spent many years in Big Horn and shared his life's experiences through his artwork. In his younger years, George was a wolfer, trapper, and soldier. In World War I, George designed a bucking horse that was selected as the emblem for the 148th Field Artillery. His 1963 mural titled *The Bozeman Trail—1863* was a gift to the Big Horn Community. George's son Junior is a member of the BHCHS. (BHCHS-BTM.)

THE ARCHIE NASH FAMILY, 1956. Archie and Alberta Nash celebrate their 25th wedding anniversary with son Alvin and daughter Elaine and her husband, Zane Hilman. Archie took many photographs of All American Indian Days and horse events under the business name of Rangeland Studios. Elaine and Zane are members of the BHCHS and have many artifacts on display in the Bozeman Trail Museum. (*Sheridan County Heritage.*)

FRED AND ALICE HILMAN. Standing under the bells that used to ring at the Hilman Dude Ranch are Fred and Alice Hilman. The dude ranch was started in 1889. The main building burned in the 1930s. The Hilman family settled on a small ranch established from the original homestead acreage. Their son Zane and his wife, Elaine, live on the ranch today. (Photograph by Archie Nash, BHCHS-BTM.)

MARY ELLEN MCWILLIAMS AND ELSA SPEAR BYRON. Mary Ellen McWilliams (left), a founder of the Fort Phil Kearney/Bozeman Trail Association, is pictured with Elsa Spear Byron, dubbed "Grand Lady of the Bozeman Trail" in 1979 by National Geographic magazine. This photograph was taken by Marilyn Bilyeu, Elsa's daughter. Mary Ellen and Marilyn are members of the BHCHS. Mary Ellen has given countless hours volunteering to preserve Sheridan County history. (Mary Ellen McWilliams.)

ROY AND NANCY GARBER. Roy and Nancy Garber stand in front of their stone house, which Roy's great-grandparents built. J.O. and Hattie Willits built a log house in 1881, then later erected this stone house in 1901. The stone house has been home to five generations of Willits and Garber families. Roy and Nancy have preserved the house, furniture, clothing, paintings, and photographs. They are members of the BHCHS. (Victor Garber family.)

THE BOZEMAN TRAIL MUSEUM. It was built in 1881 by John DeWitt. After serving as a blacksmith shop for several years, it fell into disrepair in the 1920s. This building was noted as a blacksmith shop for the Rock Creek Stage Company. The Gallatin family preserved this structure in 1936. Today, the Big Horn City Historical Society keeps the building maintained. (JS.)

WYLA AND WENDELL LOOMIS WITH BEA GALLATIN BEUF. Bea Beuf (right) was the daughter of Goelet and Edith Gallatin. Wyla and Wendell worked for the Gallatins and Bea Beuf for many years, keeping the Gallatin Ranch one of the most beautifully preserved ranches in the valley. Bea lived to be 102. Wendell passed away in 2004. All three have been supporters of the BHCHS for many years. (Dennis Loomis.)

ROBERT HELVEY, 1958. F.H. Sinclair, otherwise known as "Neckyoke Jones," stands as Robert Helvey records an interview with four Native Americans. From left to right are Charles Sitting Man, Arthur Monteith, Charles Sitting Man Jr., and Arthur Blackstone. The largest collection of interviews at the American Heritage Center is the 150 hours recorded by Robert Helvey. The American Heritage Catalog states: "The interviewees discussed a wide range of issues, including settlement and livestock operations, and the 1892 Johnson County War." (WYRM.)

THE BOZEMAN TRAIL INN. Clint Sheperd and his mother, Jeri, are the owners of the Bozeman Trail Inn. The bar and mirror are the original pieces of furniture that have been beautifully restored. It has served the town as a tavern since 1884 and was first called the Last Chance Saloon. Clint and Jeri have been members of the BHCHS. This building is listed on the National Register of Historic Places. (JS.)

HARD WORKING FRIENDS. Pictured are, from left to right, Wendell Loomis, Victor Slack, Wyla Loomis, Jackie Slack, Patty and Bud Warner, and Ralph and Ruth Blaney. These folks were involved in every service organization while they lived in Big Horn. They served in the Lions Club, volunteer fire department, Mount Hope Cemetery, 4-H, Big Horn Woman's Club, Big Horn Church, and BHCHS. These friends provided thousands of volunteer hours. (Dennis Loomis.)

JOE MEDICINE CROW AND GLENN SWEEM, 2000. They studied the Crow Indian and early archeology sites in the region. Joe Medicine Crow is a leading historian for the Crow tribe and was the first member of his tribe to earn a master's degree. He is the last traditional Crow chief. Glenn was a leading historian of this region and shared his knowledge with others. (Scott Burgan.)

THE NICKERSON FAMILY. One of the Bozeman Trail Museum's major supporters has been the Nickerson Family Foundation. Members of the foundation board are pictured. Scott and Anne Nickerson are in the front, and standing from left to right are David, Phillip, and Gregory Nickerson. Their donations have helped preserve the Elsa Spear Byron Collection at the Sheridan County Public Library's Wyoming Room. They have been BHCHS members over the years. (Nickerson family.)

HELEN GRAHAM. The author of two local Sheridan County history books and creator of the Sheridan County Fulmer Public Library's Wyoming Room is Helen Graham. She wrote *Pass Creek Country* and *Early Churches of Sheridan County, Wyoming.* She is a collector of history books and local women artists' paintings and is an amateur collector of Abe Lincoln memorabilia. She has been a member of the BHCHS for many years. (Stan Woinoski.)

CHRISTY LOVE. The Burkhart Grocery was the first business to occupy this building in 1885. It later became the meeting place for the Rebekah and Odd Fellows organizations in 1901. Christy Love remodeled it into a residence in 1978. Christy worked to have the building placed on the National Register of Historic Places in 1980. (Christy Love, taken by JS.)

CHARLIE POPOVICH. Another member of the BHCHS who has written a book that includes Big Horn City history is Charlie Popovich. He has a longtime interest in the history of schools combined with extensive research that resulted in his book titled *Sheridan County Schools—A History: With Emphasis on the Rural Schools of Sheridan County, Easy Reading.* He has also authored two other books on Sheridan County history. (Charlie Popovich.)

TOM RINGLEY. Tom is the author of four regional history books: *Rodeo Time in Sheridan Wyo: A History of the Sheridan-Wyo-Rodeo*; *Saddlestring: A History of the HF Bar Ranch*; and *When the Whistle Blows: The Turk Greenough Story*. His latest book, *Wranglin' Notes*, is on the history of the Eatons' Dude Ranch. He currently serves as a county commissioner for Sheridan County and is a member of the BHCHS. (Tom Ringley.)

ANN GORZALKA, ELSA SPEAR BYRON, AND MARGARET LOGAN. These three women have been authors of local books that are still popular today. Ann Gorzalka (left) has written *Saddlemakers of Sheridan County* and *Wyoming's Territorial Sheriffs*. Elsa (center) wrote *The Bozeman Trail Scrapbook*, and Margaret wrote *Big Horn City, Wyoming Territory 1881–1981*. Ann is a member of the BHCHS. Elsa and Margaret have passed away. They were early supporters of the BHCHS. (Elsa Spear Byron Collection at WYRM.)

JACK AND DOROTHY DOW. Jack Dow was the son of Cuthbertson "Bert" Dow and the grandson of Jack Dow. The Dow family was one of the earliest in the Little Goose Valley, homesteading northwest of Big Horn City in 1880. Their family ranch is operated today by their son, Bert. The Dow family has served on many community organizations and has been members of the BHCHS since it organized. (Victor Slack.)

SAM MORTON. *Where the Rivers Run North* and *Land of the Horse* are books relating to local history. Sam was able to capture the stories of the horsemen in northern Wyoming and southern Montana. He includes Crazy Horse, Oliver Wallop, the Moncreiffe brothers, the Gallatin family, and many of the local cowboys. He also has been a major contributor to the Bozeman Trail Museum. Sam is a member of the BHCHS. (Photo by David Lominska.)

Visit us at
arcadiapublishing.com

www.ingramcontent.com/pod-product-compliance
Lightning Source LLC
Chambersburg PA
CBHW080559110426
42813CB00006B/1347